Strong and courageous

Joshua simply explained

John D. Currid

EP BOOKS (Evangelical Press), Registered Office: 140
Coniscliffe Road, Darlington, Co Durham DL3 7RT

admin@epbooks.org
www.epbooks.org

EP Books are distributed in the USA by:
JPL Books, 3883 Linden Ave. S.E.,
Wyoming, MI 49548

order@jplbooks.com
www.jplbooks.com

First published 2011
This edition 2015

British Library Cataloguing in Publication Data

ISBN: 978-0-85234-747-8

To
Elizabeth and David

Contents

5

Part 3: The dividing (13:1–21:45)

Part 4: The serving (22:1–24:33)

Preface

The minister Charles Simeon endured great opposition and hardship when he first took up his pastorate at Trinity Church in Cambridge. He overcame it, however, and he served in that church for fifty-four years. Henry Martyn was Simeon's assistant for a time before he set sail as a missionary to India. Martyn ministered in India for only four years before his untimely death at thirty-one years of age. Martyn's short life was, in reality, a great encouragement to Charles Simeon. In four years of ministry Martyn was diligent in his labours: he preached often, established schools in India and translated the New Testament into Hindustani, Persian and Arabic. He once commissioned a portrait of himself that he sent to his friend Charles Simeon. Simeon hung the portrait over the fireplace in his study. When anyone visited Simeon in his study, he would point to the portrait and say, 'See that blessed man. No one looks at me as he does. He never takes his eyes off me, and he seems always to be saying, "The years are short. Be serious. Be in earnest. Don't trifle; don't trifle."' Then Simeon would say, 'And I won't trifle; I won't trifle.'

In this study of the book of Joshua, I have tried not to trifle. Rather, I have attempted to be diligent to get to the heart of the book and its message. I do hope that the church today will benefit from these labours. I want to thank my two research assistants for their excellent work in editing this material: Rachel Icard and Lacy Larson. Your hard work has not gone unnoticed. I also want to thank my wife Nancy for always being a source of encouragement in my writing. I dedicate this book to my two children, Elizabeth and David. I pray that you would hold fast to the promises of God as you journey to the land of promise.

John Currid

Introduction

Many years ago an acquaintance told me that he was having great difficulty in selling his home. It had been on the market so long that he was beginning to panic. He had purchased another home and he was barely meeting the two mortgage payments. He then told me that he and his family had done a 'Joshua march' the night before. I asked him what that was. He said that he and his family held hands and marched around their house seven times. I couldn't help myself and I blurted out, 'Were you trying to sell it, or knock it down?'

That story is perhaps humorous, but it also speaks to a sad reality. People often easily misread and misapply the book of Joshua. I once heard a sermon on Joshua 10:10, which reads, 'And the LORD threw them into a panic before Israel, who struck them with a great blow at Gibeon and chased them by the way of the ascent of Beth-horon and struck them as far as Azekah and Makkedah.' The preacher thundered forth his application of this text to the congregation by saying, 'What is the ascent in your life? What things do you need to strike from your life?' Now, almost instinctively, listeners know there is something not quite right about that interpretation. And, indeed, it is allegorical, and allegory as a method of interpretation needs to be shunned at almost all costs. But it is a common way of understanding a book like Joshua in literature and in the pulpit.

Why is the book of Joshua so often mishandled? I believe the answer to that question is really quite simple: the book is written in historical narrative. That literary style is not difficult to understand, but it is very hard to apply to one's audience or congregation. Now, don't get me wrong. I am convinced and insist that proper application of narrative is possible and warranted; however, it takes extensive labour and mining to uncover the riches of the text. So let's turn to consider some of the more important principles necessary for the appropriate interpretation and application of a historical narrative such as Joshua.

Literary genre

The writers of Scripture employ various genres, or literary styles of composition, in their penning of the Bible. For example, the author of the book of Numbers uses 'narrative (4:1–3), poetry (21:17–18), prophecy (24:3–9), victory song (21:27–30), prayer (12:13), blessing (6:24–26), lampoon (22:22–35), diplomatic letter (20:14–19), civil law (27:1–11), cultic law (15:17–21), oracular decision (15:32–36), census list (26:1–51), temple archive (7:10–88), itinerary (33:1–49)'.[1] The same is true for the book of Joshua: it includes poetry (6:26; 10:12–13), conquest itineraries (10:29–42; 11:1–23), land grants (15:1–19:51), a covenant document (24:1–28) and obituaries (24:29–33). The dominant literary format for Joshua, however, is historical narrative.

Literary analysis is a field of study that deals with what Robert Alter calls 'the artful use of language' in a particular genre.[2] This includes such conventions of Hebrew writing as wordplays, plays on ideas, imagery, sound, syntax, and many other things. There are various stages of the 'artful' use of Hebrew language in a biblical narrative like the book of Joshua. We will consider these stages briefly, beginning with the smallest and proceeding to the larger and more elaborate.

1. *Leitwort (a leading word, or keyword)*

The German term *Leitwort* refers to a word, or root-word, that appears repeatedly throughout a passage. By observing the repetitions closely, the reader may derive the meaning and significance of the text in a more striking manner. Let's turn to an example in the narrative of 1 Samuel 15:1–31.

This episode describes a confrontation between Samuel, the prophet of Israel, and Saul, the king of Israel, with regard to the annihilation of the Amalekites. The dominant *Leitwort* in this story is the Hebrew word *qol*, which means 'voice'. It first appears in the opening verse of the chapter, in which Samuel orders Saul to listen to 'the voice of the words of the LORD'.³ Saul is to obey God's voice by destroying all that belongs to Amalek (v. 3). Later Samuel confronts Saul about the situation with Amalek, and Saul claims to have obeyed the Lord's command (v. 13). Samuel, however, is dismayed because he, literally, hears 'the voice' of sheep and 'the voice' of oxen (v. 14). After Samuel is told that the Israelites spared the best of the animals, he chides Saul by saying (literally), 'Why then did you not listen to the voice of the LORD?' (v. 19). Saul counters by saying (again, literally), 'I did listen to the voice of the LORD' (v. 20). Samuel responds, 'Has the LORD as great delight in burnt offerings and sacrifices, as in obeying the voice of the LORD?' (v. 22). Then, in verse 24, Saul makes a final defence for his actions: he says he acted this way 'because I feared the people and obeyed their voice'.

In this passage there occurs a symphony of voices. The Lord speaks; the animals speak; the Israelite people speak; and Samuel speaks. The core of the meaning of the story is: which voice will Saul listen to? The author's use of the *Leitwort* drives home this point.

2. Leitphrase (a leading, or key phrase)

Narrative texts are often more complicated than merely having one *Leitwort*. Many passages will contain more than one such term, and sometimes a phrase (*Leitphrase*), rather than a single word, may dominate a text. For example, in Genesis 39:1–6 a number of *Leitwörter* and one *Leitphrase* appear in the text. The leading words are 'all' (five times), 'house' (five times), 'hand' (four times) and 'success' (twice). The phrase, 'the LORD was with Joseph', occurs twice in these verses. The storyline concerns and describes Joseph's servitude to Potiphar, his Egyptian master.

Later in the same chapter we read about Joseph's imprisonment, and how he is treated by the Egyptian jailer (Genesis 39:19–23). Interestingly, the same leading words appear here as in the earlier account: 'all' (three times), 'house' (four times), 'hand' (twice) and 'success' (once). In addition, the key phrase, 'the LORD was with Joseph', is present twice. The point of these repetitions is to underscore a pattern: because the Lord is with Joseph, the patriarch's human master places all in his hands, and he is successful with it. This essential pattern prevails to the ultimate degree when Pharaoh places all the house of Egypt into Joseph's hands (Genesis 41:37–45).

3. Leitmotif (a leading scene, or recurring theme)

A perplexing issue for interpreters is the fact that in biblical narrative, the same story, more or less, appears more than once in the literature. For instance, in the book of Genesis the motif, 'she is my sister', occurs three times (Genesis 12:10-20; 20:1-18; 26:6-11). It appears on the first two occasions with regard to Abraham, and the third time with Isaac. The common answer to such repetition is that the duplication of narrative is to be attributed to the duplication of sources. In other words, different sources use the same story for different episodes and purposes. In reality, that understanding is faulty because a type-scene, or leitmotif, is at the very heart of biblical narrative. It is one of the primary ways in which a biblical writer relates his material.

Let me give an example. Genesis 19:1-29 presents the story of Sodom and Gomorrah. It records the tale of the wickedness of the Sodomites as they attempt to do harm to the angels who are assisting Lot. Almost exactly the same storyline appears in Judges 19:22-30, in which the tribe of Benjamin deals with a visiting Levite in the city of Gibeah. Even some of the vocabulary and phraseology of the two stories are exactly alike (see, for example, Judges 19:22 and Genesis 19:4; Judges 19:23 and Genesis 19:7; Judges 19:24 and Genesis 19:8). Why would the writer of Judges relay the historical episode in Gibeah in such a way as to remind the reader of the historical event of Sodom? The answer is like a thunder-clap: the Benjamites are acting just like the pagan Sodomites! The morality of the people of Israel has really sunk to an all-time low by the later stages of the book of Judges.

Another example of a leitmotif is the 'barren wife' scene that occurs frequently throughout Scripture. The motif is that of an Israelite woman unable to bear children, and then by miraculous means she conceives and bears a son. The son then becomes a leader or deliverer of the people of God. It appears first in Genesis 11:27-30 with barren Sarah; Isaac is born miraculously to the aged Abraham and his wife. This theme repeats in Genesis

25:20-21 (Rebekah); Genesis 29:31 (Rachel); Judges 13:2 (Samson's mother) and 1 Samuel 1:2 (Hannah). The leitmotif, of course, reaches its climax in the virgin birth of the Saviour Jesus Christ!

4. Miscellaneous elements

There are many other elements of the skilful use of language that can help the reader understand a narrative text properly. For example, when we study the Bible we ought to be aware of the literary use of a 'foil'. A foil is a 'character that stands in contrast to another character, thereby highlighting one or more of the latter's characteristics or traits'.[4] A good example of a foil is seen in Genesis 38, a chapter that interrupts the story of Joseph. Why is this story of Judah, one of deceit and sexual immorality, placed in such a disruptive place? It is for the purpose of providing a foil: Judah marries a Canaanite, and after her death he has sexual relations with a woman he thinks is a prostitute. Joseph, in contrast, does not fall victim to sexual temptation (Genesis 39:1-10). In support of this contrast, Genesis 38 is devoid of any mention of the Lord; there is total spiritual silence. However, in Genesis 39, four times it is stated that 'the LORD was with Joseph' (vv. 2,3,21,23).

Other literary techniques of narrative will be discussed as we comment on the text of the book of Joshua. These include such elements as chiasmus, inclusion and typology.

Summary outline

The book of Joshua can be outlined in the following general fashion:

1:1–5:12	The crossing
5:13–12:24	The seizing

13:1–21:45	The dividing
22:1–24:33	The serving

This structure is based on the dominant *Leitwort* that appears in each of these major sections of the book.[5] In part 1, the verb 'to cross', or 'pass over', occurs repeatedly (see, e.g., 1:2,11; 3:11,16; 4:5,13,22,23; 5:1). The verb 'to take', 'seize', or 'receive' is common in the second section (e.g., 7:11; 11:19; 13:8; 18:7). A recurring verb in the third section is 'to divide' (e.g., 18:2,5,6,9). And, finally, the noun 'servant' and the verb 'to serve' stand out in the final part of the book (e.g., 22:2,4,5,27; 24:14,15,16,29).

The structure of the book is significant. The first three sections–crossing, seizing and dividing–are all done by divine initiative. It is the Lord who commands and leads. The final section is Israel's response to God's work in the first three parts of the book. The people of God take an oath that they will indeed serve this God who delivered them from Egypt, brought them across the Jordan River, led the conquest of Canaan and allotted the land to their various tribes.

The theme of Joshua

Clearly the central theme of the book of Joshua is the truth that God is a promise-keeper. Well over five hundred years before these recorded events, God pledged to Abraham that 'To your offspring I will give this land' (Genesis 12:7). The land he is referring to is Canaan. From that time onward, up to the period of the conquest, God repeatedly makes the same promise to his people (see Genesis 13:15; 15:18; 17:8; 24:7; 26:3–4; 28:13; 35:12; Exodus 3:8; Numbers 34:2; Deuteronomy 34:4; cf. Acts 7:5). This promise occurs so frequently in the Pentateuch that it seems to sum up the theme of the literature.

The writer of the book of Joshua recognizes the importance of this theme. The fulfilment of God's promises of a land is central to the book. He begins the book with it (1:2–3) and brings to a close Joshua's final charge to Israel's leaders with it (23:14–15). And the promises of God are found throughout the book as having been fulfilled (see, e.g., 22:4; 23:5,10).

The truth that God fulfils his promise of a land for Israel also has great implications for the believer today, and that is one of the principal applications of the book of Joshua. Those who truly belong to God's people—that is, those who have been redeemed by the blood of Christ—will inherit a land. However, that land is not the dry and dusty land in the Middle East today. Rather, the apostle Peter tells us that God 'has caused us to be born again to a living hope through the resurrection of Jesus Christ from the dead, to an inheritance that is imperishable, undefiled, and unfading, kept in heaven for you' (1 Peter 1:3–4). We as believers have God's promise of an eternal inheritance and the possession of an eternal land that is real, earthy and substantial. And, like Israel, we shall indeed receive our inheritance because God is a promise-keeper!

Let's now open up the text of the book, and let's attempt to understand and cling to its gripping message.

Part 1:

The crossing (1:1–5:12)

1

Be strong and courageous

Please read Joshua 1:1–9

One of the great preachers of Scottish Presbyterianism in the seventeenth century was John Livingstone (1603–72). When he was a young man in his twenties he doubted whether he had a call to the ministry; he had a great fear that God had not set him apart to that work. When he was twenty-seven years old he still had no ministerial charge. A neighbouring minister one day engaged him to preach on a Sunday at his church in Shotts. The morning of the sermon Livingstone had such a fit of fear and panic that he sought to flee before the service. He took heart, however, knowing that fleeing would show distrust for God, and courageously went forth and preached on Ezekiel 36:25–26. Five hundred people ascribed their conversion to that sermon.[1]

From an earthly standpoint, Israel had multiple reasons to be in great fear at the beginning of the book of Joshua. Moses had just died (Deuteronomy 34). It was he who had led the deliverance out of Egypt, brought down the law from Sinai and taken the people to the very edges of the land of promise. He had been the covenant mediator—that is, the man who 'stood in the breach' between the sinful, unholy nation and the Holy One of Israel (Psalm 106:23). Now he is no longer alive to lead them, having been buried by the very hand of God. They are poised to enter and capture the land of Canaan, but how can they do those things without a leader?

In addition, Israel is facing formidable opposition in Canaan. The peoples of the land are well entrenched inside major cities that have strong defensive systems. During the Late Bronze Age, for example, the city of Hazor had a huge double casemated wall encircling the site.[2] Thus, we see a wandering people set to engage a mostly urbanized, settled and strong population, which has been in the land for centuries. Such a scenario would, on a human level, cause them to lose heart easily. An indication of Israel's panic before such odds is clearly seen in their response to the report of the spies in Numbers 14:1–4.

What will happen now that Moses is dead? How will the people respond? How will they deal with their fear? How will they face the looming danger that lies across the Jordan River?

The Lord's command (1:1–2)

The first word of the Hebrew text is properly translated as 'and it was', or 'and it came to pass'; it is a term that indicates historical sequence and connection to something that went before. The book of Deuteronomy had ended with the death of Moses, and now the Lord turns to speak to Joshua, the successor to Moses. Joshua is called the 'minister', or 'assistant' of Moses; this word, or its related verb, is employed in the Old Testament of a chief servant or one who acts as a right-hand man (Genesis 39:4; 40:4), and sometimes specifically of one who stands next in line for a position (1 Kings 19:21). Joshua has been trained for this very task. Therefore, the opening answer to the fear of the people is that *God has appointed a replacement for Moses*: the new leader and covenant mediator is Joshua (see his commissioning in Deuteronomy 31:1–8).

We need to recognize that God is the constant one in this story. People come and go. Leaders come and go. But the Lord and his word remain for ever. When George Müller was asked, 'What, Mr Müller, will become of the Orphan Houses, when you are removed?' Müller replied, 'The Orphan Houses, and the land belonging to them, are vested in the hand of eleven trustees...' The response was: 'But where will you find the man who will carry on the work in the same spirit in which you do, trusting only in God for everything that in any way is needed in connection with the work?' Müller answered, 'When the Lord shall have been pleased to remove me from my post, He will prove that He was not dependent on me, and that He can easily raise up another servant of His to act on the same principles on which I have sought to carry on this work.' Thus Israel is not to set her chief affections and trust on a leader, but on the constant God.

The second answer to Israel's fear is that *God had deeded the land of promise to the people of Israel.* Three times in the passage God employs the verb 'to give' (1:2,3,6). Canaan is simply a gift from the hand of God. And, furthermore, the giving of the land to them is a fulfilment of God's promise to the sons of Israel that he made as far back as the time of Abraham. In Genesis 12, Abram 'came to the land of Canaan' (v. 5), and God appeared to him and promised, 'To your offspring I will give this land' (v. 7).

God repeatedly made this promise to the patriarchs (Genesis 13:15; 15:18; 17:8) and to the people of Israel when they were enslaved in Egypt (Exodus 6:8). Now is the time when God will keep his promise!

The inheritance (1:3–4)

The amount and extent of the land that God is giving to Israel is now defined. The Lord first says that their inheritance will include 'every place that the sole of your foot will tread upon'. This metaphorical expression in the Old Testament refers to the practice of gaining formal title to a land by walking through it (see Deuteronomy 11:24). In ancient Near-Eastern literature, examples exist of kings who walk through lands in order to demonstrate their ownership and authority over those areas.[3]

In verse 4, God provides greater detail concerning the size of Israel's land inheritance, yet it is only a general outline of the territory included. Their land will extend from 'the wilderness', which obviously refers to the desert lands to the south of Canaan, to the Euphrates River, which lies to the north-east of Canaan. The western boundary of the inheritance will be the 'Great Sea', where the sun sets—namely, the Mediterranean Sea. For a more specific delineation of Israel's inheritance boundaries in the land of promise, see Numbers 34:1–12.

Land grants with specific boundaries are common features of ancient Near-Eastern covenants.[4] Joshua 1:1–4 looks like a royal land grant typically made by a king (here, the Lord) to a vassal or subordinate (here, Israel).

The Immanuel principle (1:5)

Another reason is now given why Israel should not be afraid, but rather should forge ahead and conquer the land of Canaan.

No man 'shall ... stand before' Joshua all the days of his life; this Hebrew idiom means that no one will be able to withstand Joshua and Israel or defeat them (see Deuteronomy 7:24). No enemy will be able to oppose Joshua because the Lord is with him as he was with Moses. This is the Immanuel principle, in which the term 'Immanuel' literally means, 'God is with us.' The presence of the sovereign God with his people should, in fact, drown out Israel's debilitating fear and embolden them to act. Again, Yahweh is constant, giving and trustworthy; therefore, the people should not be afraid.

Be strong and courageous (1:6–9)

How are Joshua and Israel to react to the command of God that they cross into the land of promise? First, the Lord, using imperatival forms, says three times that the people are to be 'strong and courageous'; the Hebrew language often employs repetition for the purpose of emphasis. Israel is to respond to God's commands with valour, daring and fortitude. They are in no way to be passive, but they are to prepare themselves, take heart and have backbone to fight.

Secondly, God demands that Israel obey his Scriptures that he gave in the Torah. The people are about to enter a land full of wickedness and violence, and their primary safeguard against the ways and means of the ungodly is God's Word. The Torah, in fact, is not to depart from their mouths, and the people are to 'meditate on it day and night'. The latter phrase is an example of a merism, a set of opposites that are all-inclusive. Thus, the Israelites are to ponder God's Word and its application to them diligently and consistently as they enter the land of promise. Remember what Moses said to the people as they stood in the plains of Moab looking across the Jordan River at the land of promise: 'Take to heart all the words by which I am warning you today, that you may command them to your children, that they may be careful to do all the words of this law. For it is no empty word for you, but your very life, and by this word you shall live long in the land that you are going over the Jordan to possess' (Deuteronomy 32:46–47).

Points to ponder

1. God's threefold provision for his people

The people of Israel are facing an overwhelming task at the beginning of the book of Joshua. God has commanded that they cross over the Jordan River and capture the land of promise, which is filled with foes. Yet God has not left the people to themselves to carry out their duty. He has equipped Israel to stand up to their enemies in three ways: firstly, God promises to be with Israel as they enter the land of Canaan; secondly, he raises strong leadership in the person of Joshua; and, thirdly, he gives the people his Word to stand on and to live by.

God continues to equip his people in the church in these very same ways. When Jesus gave the church the commission to 'make disciples of all nations', he said, 'And behold, I am with you always, to the end of the age' (Matthew 28:19,20). The Lord is with his people. And he continues to establish strong leadership in the church; for example, when Paul spoke to the elders at Ephesus he encouraged them to take care of the flock, in 'which the Holy Spirit has made you overseers' (Acts 20:28). And, indeed, the church has the Word of God, which is 'living and active, sharper than any two-edged sword' (Hebrews 4:12). For, 'All Scripture is breathed out by God and profitable for teaching, for reproof, for correction, and for training in righteousness, that the man of God may be competent, equipped for every good work' (2 Timothy 3:16–17).

2. Courage in the face of trials

God's people, whether in Joshua's day or today, are not to fear, but they are to be 'strong and courageous'. When Martin Luther was travelling to the Diet of Worms, where he was to go on trial before the Roman Catholic Church, he was told that he would be given no safe conduct. As Luther neared the city for the trial, a friendly priest warned him, 'Do not enter the city!' But Luther, undismayed, looked at the priest and said, 'Even should there be as many devils in Worms as tiles upon the housetops, still I would enter it.' Luther claimed, 'I was undaunted... I feared nothing.'

In the midst of those great trials, Luther responded with great courage. During the darkest times, he would say, 'Come, let us sing the 46th Psalm, and let them do their worst.' On the basis of Psalm 46, Luther wrote the awe-inspiring hymn 'A Mighty Fortress is our God':

And though this world, with devils filled,
   should threaten to undo us,
We will not fear, for God has willed,
   his truth to triumph through us.
The prince of darkness grim—
     we tremble not for him;
His rage we can endure,
     for, lo! his doom is sure;
One little word shall fell him.

2

Joshua takes command

Please read Joshua 1:10–18

Thomas Adams once commented that 'True obedience has no lead at its heels.'[1] And that is a reality we see with regard to the person of Joshua in this passage. His response is immediate; there is no hesitation, questioning, or lingering. He does not enter into dialogue with God, but simply obeys the divine command. He acts upon the orders that the Lord has given to him. Joshua is a faithful, obedient servant. He well echoes the sentiments of Martin Luther, who said, 'I know not the way he leads me, but well do I know my Guide. What have I to fear?'[2]

Joshua gives orders (1:10–11)

Joshua first executes his leadership role by commanding the military leaders to prepare the people of Israel for the conquest of the land of Canaan. All the tribes have a mere three days to equip their armies for an assault on the land. This amount of time gives the people little opportunity to linger or to be idle; prolonging the inevitable attack could perhaps arouse fear, gossip and rebellion. It is time to obey the divine orders and to be determined and diligent in so doing.

The term 'provisions' is primarily used in the Old Testament of supplies of food; thus, the Hebrew warriors are to prepare enough rations to sustain them in war. The specific amount of food to be gathered and prepared is unspecified. When the Israelites came out of Egypt, the text declares that they had not 'prepared any provisions for themselves' (Exodus 12:39). They had to leave Egypt quickly, and they had no time for preparation. The same language is now used of Israel as the people are about to storm the land of Canaan, only at this juncture they have time to prepare.

Joshua commands the Transjordanian tribes (1:12–15)

Joshua now turns specifically to speak to the tribes who are settling in the land of Transjordan: these are the tribes of Reuben, Gad and the half-tribe of Manasseh. Joshua calls them to remember the promise they had made to Moses. The agreement is found in Numbers 32. In that passage, the Transjordanian tribes swore to take up arms and go before the other tribes into Canaan, saying, 'We will not return to our homes until each of the people of Israel has gained his inheritance' (Numbers 32:18). Joshua is now calling on these tribes to keep the word they gave to Moses.

Points to ponder

1. The Lord's promises to his people are sure

Centuries before the present episode, God had pledged to Abraham, saying, 'To your offspring I will give this land' (Genesis

12:7). And he repeated that promise to Abraham (Genesis 13:15; 15:18; 17:8), to the other patriarchs (Genesis 26:4; 28:13; 35:12), and to the Israelites in Egypt (Exodus 6:8). And now, as Israel prepares for war, they are on the very brink of realizing God's promises coming to pass. This reality should, indeed, encourage the people as they face the trials of war.

In the seventeenth century a man named Richard Cameron, a Covenanter, was martyred. 'Before the hangman set head and hands on the bloodstained Netherbow Port, the fingers pointing grimly upwards on either side of the head, a hero saint lying in prison was shown them. He was Alan Cameron, Covenanter.'[3] The guards cruelly asked him, 'Do you know them?' He kissed the body parts, and said, 'I know them, I know them. They are my son's, my own dear son's. It is the Lord. Good is the will of the Lord, who cannot wrong me nor mine, but has made goodness and mercy to follow us all our days.'[4] Indeed, God does not abandon his people even in times of war and death, but he is true to his word to them.

> Surely goodness and mercy shall follow me
>   all the days of my life,
> and I shall dwell in the house of the LORD
>   for ever
>
> (Psalm 23:6).

George Müller made the following statement when preaching on Psalm 23:6:

This brings before us what the child of God finds, in acquaintance with Christ. Not merely entering into what God has given him in Christ Jesus; not merely having to say, 'My cup runneth over; I am brimful of happiness.' But,

'I have almost more than I can bear. I find it so pleasant, so exceedingly pleasant, this way of going on, I can never get into another position any more. I will remain in the house of my Heavenly Father for ever.' ... Not merely so. But 'Goodness and mercy shall follow me all the days of my life.' I shall now be for ever and ever a happy man, and I will remain in the presence of my Father; I will not leave His house any more, because I have found it so very, very precious to be a child of God.

2. The antidote to fear is obedience to God and his Word

Believers are called to run the race of life with endurance, fortitude and Scripture. Christians are not to lose heart, be gripped with fear, or shrink from their task. John Flavel once remarked, 'The upright soul abhors to flinch from his duty, let come on him what will.'[5] The Bible, indeed, encourages believers to 'run with endurance the race that is set before us' (Hebrews 12:1). 'The course may be long, treacherous, and uphill, but that does not matter. For we do not run the race in our own power, but "I can do all things through him who strengthens me" (Philippians 4:13).'[6]

3. Unity among God's people

At the outset of the book of Joshua the reader ought to be struck by the unity of God's people as they prepare to face the enemy. In Numbers 32 Moses had rebuked the Transjordanian tribes, assuming that they did not plan to participate in the conquest of Canaan (vv. 6–7). By not helping the other tribes, they would cause a negative result. 'It is an issue of *morale*; the other tribes will become discouraged and they will have a sense of abandonment.'[7]

Was Moses fair in making such an accusation? Yes. Indeed,

a similar accusation is brought against those tribes in Joshua 22:13–20. The Transjordanian tribes had built an altar, and the other tribes viewed this act as those three tribes having gone their own way. Another incident occurs in Judges 5:17. There Deborah accuses the Hebrews in Transjordan of staying put rather than participating in a war against the Canaanites. This 'disunity appears to have been systemic for the Transjordanian tribes'.[8]

In any event, at the beginning of the book of Joshua we see a true and real unity of the people of God as the Transjordanian tribes prepare to lead the troops into Canaan. Ralph Davis appropriately comments: 'One can detect implications here for the doctrine and practice of the church—unity among God's people is no idle luxury.'[9] The apostle Paul encourages the church to be 'eager to maintain the unity of the Spirit in the bond of peace. There is one body and one Spirit—just as you were called to the one hope that belongs to your call—one Lord, one faith, one baptism, one God and Father of all, who is over all and through all and in all' (Ephesians 4:3–6). The unity displayed in the book of Joshua is short-lived, however; the period of the judges soon follows, in which 'Everyone did what was right in his own eyes' (Judges 17:6; 21:25). The church similarly undergoes seasons of unity and disunity; the church of the twenty-first century appears to be in a time of fragmentation.

3

Reconnoitring the land

Please read Joshua 2:1–24

t the beginning of the Gospel of Matthew, the apostle presents 'the genealogy of Jesus Christ, the son of David, the son of Abraham' (Matthew 1:1). Part of this ancestry of Jesus reads as follows: '... and Salmon the father of Boaz by Rahab, and Boaz the father of Obed by Ruth, and Obed the father of Jesse, and Jesse the father of David the king' (Matthew 1:5–6).

The inclusion of women in a genealogy is striking because it is so rare in Old Testament genealogies. Five women are mentioned in the genealogy of Jesus; four of them are cited by name, and one is simply called 'the wife of Uriah' (Matthew 1:6). The named women are Tamar, Rahab, Ruth and Mary; Bathsheba, of course, is the unnamed wife of Uriah. All five of these women have questionable backgrounds from the point of view of Jewish law: Tamar was accused of harlotry

(Genesis 38:24–25); Ruth was from the pagan Moabites (Ruth 1:4); Bathsheba had committed adultery with David (2 Samuel 11); and Mary the mother of Jesus was with child before having a husband (Matthew 1:18). Rahab has double ignominy: she was not only a Canaanite, but also a prostitute (2:1). That these women are included in the genealogy of Jesus indicates that no one is beyond the pale when it comes to God's saving grace. As the apostle Paul says, 'There is neither Jew nor Greek, there is neither slave nor free, there is neither male nor female, for you are all one in Christ Jesus' (Galatians 3:28). In addition, the inclusion of these women (and, indeed, many of the men) demonstrates that God delights in bestowing his mercy and grace upon people in the most unexpected way and in the most unlikely circumstances. Do we really believe that our sin or our circumstances can stand in the way of God's work of salvation? Indeed, it cannot.

It is also important to note that Rahab the Canaanite is the great-great-grandmother of David, and that Ruth the Moabitess is his great-grandmother (see Ruth 4:21–22). Rahab is thus an important person in the genealogical line that leads to the greatest king of Israel and, ultimately, to the King of kings. Indeed, the author of the book of Hebrews recognizes Rahab's prominence when he writes, 'By faith Rahab the prostitute did not perish with those who were disobedient, because she had given a friendly welcome to the spies' (Hebrews 11:31). Rahab, the Canaanite prostitute, was—a woman of faith!

D. Martyn Lloyd-Jones tells the story of an extraordinary event in the early days of his ministry at his first church in Aberavon. One Sunday morning, as 'the Doctor' was about to preach, he noticed that the inside of the church had become unbearably hot. So he stood up and asked the elders to open the windows of the church to let in some cool air. He then began to preach. Just at that time the most notorious drunk and bully of the town, an extremely ruthless man, was walking by the church to go down to the pub in order to tank up for the day. As he was passing the church, he heard Lloyd-Jones preaching through the open windows, and there and then he fell on his knees in repentance. We need to realize that no person is beyond God's reach if God so wills and delights to bring him to saving faith. No one is too far gone, and Rahab is one of the prime examples of this truth from the Old Testament.

Spies in the land (2:1)

Joshua now sends two of his men to search out the land and, in particular, the area of Jericho. Here, for the first time, we receive a clue as to where specifically the Israelites will begin their attack on Canaan. The men are sent from the site of Shittim, which is commonly identified with Abel-shittim located at the modern Tell al-Kafren. This site sits approximately twelve miles directly east of Jericho on the other side of the Jordan River.

The spies are to search out the land 'secretly'; this term in Hebrew literally means 'silently', and so they are to explore the land without being detected. To do this the men go to the house of a prostitute. What better place to go to be undiscovered? A *modus operandi* of a house of prostitution is to keep quiet about and guard the names of its clientele! The name of the harlot is Rahab. And the two spies rest and lie down in her house.

City gossip (2:2–3)

Word of the spies' clandestine exploration somehow finds its way to the king of Jericho. It is interesting that the leader of Jericho is called a 'king', because this certainly reflects the political stage of Canaan as we know it from documents of the time. According to the Amarna Letters, Canaan was divided into a series of city states, 'and these city states held quite large regions under their sway'.[1] In these letters, the local city-state ruler is known as a 'prince' but, 'In writing about one another they often speak of one another as "king", and the king of Hazor even calls himself this in the preamble to letter 227.'[2] In any event, it is this chief leader of the Jericho city state who hears of the Israelite spies in his city.

The term 'behold' is the opening word spoken to the king; it functions as an exclamation expressing an immediate need or attention. It is what Lambdin calls the 'here-and-now-ness'.[3] In other words, whoever is reporting to the king is aware of a lurking and present danger of Israelite spies in their midst.

The king of Jericho is somehow able to ascertain that the spies are hiding in the house of Rahab the prostitute. So, apparently, he sends messengers or soldiers to confront Rahab and to order her to produce the Israelite spies.

The great escape (2:4–7)

Rahab obviously senses an impending danger of the spies being found out. So, she 'hid them' on her roof among the stalks of flax piled there. The Hebrew verb for 'hid' literally means 'to bury', and thus the two Hebrew spies are buried deep inside the flax. Flax was used in antiquity to produce linen thread, but the flax had to be completely dried before it could be employed in that way. Part of the process was that flax stalks would be laid out to dry on the roof of a house. This would have been a common practice for many, if not most, of the households in Jericho.

When the soldiers confront Rahab, she wisely does not deny that the men had come to her house. Rather, she admits it, but then counters by saying that she had no idea who they were. The prostitute then tells a downright lie by saying that the Israelites are no longer in her house. They have left Jericho, and she does not know where they went. It is noteworthy that Rahab is commended in the New Testament for her actions in this situation (Hebrews 11:31; James 2:25). However, it needs to be observed that in neither New Testament text is she acclaimed because of her lying; rather, she is acclaimed because 'she had given a friendly welcome to the spies'.

The soldiers believe the report given by Rahab, and so they pursue the spies towards the east to the Jordan River. Of course, the men of Jericho know that the Israelite camp is across the Jordan in the plains of Moab, and that the spies would need to go in that direction to get back. The guards of the city of Jericho shut the gates after the pursuers leave —perhaps they are suspicious either that the spies might still be in the city, or that they might covertly come back if the gates were left open.

Rahab's request (2:8–13)

After the immediate danger has passed, Rahab goes up on the roof of her house to talk with the Israelite spies. And she says to them with great certainty, 'I know that the LORD has given you the land …' The word she uses for 'LORD' is 'Yahweh'—that is, the Hebrew covenantal name that God revealed to Moses at the burning bush. So here is a pagan prostitute who does 'know' that the land of Canaan has been deeded by Yahweh to the Israelites. Often this verb in Hebrew carries the idea of intimate knowledge; in other words, Rahab has a deep, personal conviction that what she has just said is true.

Rahab also admits that the peoples of Canaan are afraid of the approaching Israelites, and that because of the Hebrew presence the people's strength and confidence have 'melted away'. This latter verb is used in the Old Testament of someone losing heart, or becoming faint of heart. Soon after the Israelites had gone through the midst of the Red Sea, Moses led them in a song that anticipated this reaction on the part of the Canaanites: 'all the inhabitants of Canaan have melted away' (Exodus 15:15). And that is exactly what is happening as the Israelites prepare to pounce on the land.

Rahab explains why there is such fear (2:10). The Canaanites have heard that Yahweh has acted mightily by miraculously drying up the Red Sea and bringing Israel through it. When Jethro, Moses' father-in-law, heard the same story he also, like Rahab, came under great conviction: 'Now I know that the LORD is greater than all gods, because in this affair they dealt arrogantly with the people' (Exodus 18:11). The reality is that most non-Israelites did not respond positively to that story. Even more fear is elicited when the Canaanites hear what happened to the two Transjordanian kings, Sihon and Og (recorded in Numbers 21:21–35). Those kings had been placed 'under the ban'; this terminology refers to an object that is consecrated to total destruction (see 6:17,21,24). Sometimes it can refer to a partial ban, as appears to be the case with Sihon and Og: Israel 'defeated him and his sons and all his people, until he had no survivor left' (Numbers 21:35). But Israel kept all the cities of these kings and the materials and things found in them (Numbers 21:25).

In Joshua 2:11, Rahab repeats the points she made in verses 9–10 for emphasis. She declares a second time that their hearts had melted and their spirits had plummeted when they heard the stories of Israel. Then Rahab makes a stunning personal confession: she declares that Yahweh is the 'God in the heavens above and on the earth beneath'. The two words 'heaven' and 'earth' serve as a merism—that is, two opposites that are all-inclusive. Thus, her proclamation is stating that Yahweh is God over all. This assertion is especially striking in the light of the Canaanite belief in polytheism and of their personification of their gods in the very elements of creation.[4]

Rahab then makes a pact with the spies (2:12–13). She asks that they would 'deal kindly' with her and her family in the same way that she has 'dealt kindly' with them. The Hebrew word is *chesed*; it is often used in covenant contexts, and is properly translated as 'covenant loyalty'. Rahab is asking that these Israelite spies would 'swear' to a covenant with her. She also requests a true sign—that is, a physical sign, or covenantal witness to the agreement.

The spies' oath (2:14)

A covenant between people is often a bond in blood—that is, it extends to life and death. This is the case here as the men announce, 'Our life for yours', if they are not true to the covenantal agreement. Interestingly, the 'yours' is a plural pronoun which indicates that the spies' promise extends to Rahab's family. The men further vow that they will 'deal kindly'—that is, swear covenant fidelity—with her.

Rahab makes good their escape (2:15–16)

Rahab helps the spies to escape by dropping a rope from her window to the outside of the city. Her house was 'built into the city wall'. This latter clause may indicate that the city had a casemated wall system which had an outer fortification wall running parallel with an inner wall that also served to provide rooms for the inhabitants of the city. This type of construction is well known and has been preserved from the Late Bronze and Iron Ages of Palestine.[5]

Rahab then tells the spies to flee to the hill country until the Jericho soldiers return from their pursuit. In verse 7, the soldiers are pictured as chasing after the spies 'on the way to the Jordan', which is *east* of Jericho. Rahab directs the spies to travel to the hill country and lie low there—the hill country is to the *west* of Jericho. After three days, the way will be clear, and then the spies can travel east, cross the Jordan and reunite with the camp of Israel in Moab.

The final oath (2:17–21)

The spies now provide details to the covenant that they have made with Rahab. They are specific with regard to what she is required to do—if she deviates from the stipulations, then they will be 'guiltless', or 'innocent', if the oath is broken. The men tell her this twice, once at the beginning of their address (2:17) and once at its close (2:20). This is what grammarians call an *inclusio*—that is, a literary technique that marks the beginning and end of a section; its primary purpose is emphasis. The spies stress the fact that Rahab's obedience to the stipulations of the covenant is a necessary condition of it.

Rahab is required to hang a scarlet cord from her window. This cord, which is a rope and not a thread, serves as a sign to the Israelite forces not to kill those who are inside that particular house. She is to gather her extended family into the house, and thus they will be protected. However, if anyone from her extended family is outside the house, that person will not be protected by the sign of the scarlet cord.

This story is reminiscent of the Passover event in Egypt (Exodus 11:1–13:16). In that episode, God tells his people to put the blood of the Passover lamb on the doors of the houses in which they live. God will pass through Egypt bringing a plague, and those who are in the houses with the blood on the doorposts will not be harmed.

In the tenth plague, God will again make a distinction between his people and Pharaoh's people. Those who belong to Yahweh will bear upon their houses the sign of blood, and they will not be struck by the plague. Those who do not mark their homes with blood will suffer the plague. [6]

In the case of Rahab, the scarlet cord serves as the sign that all who reside within the house will be protected and delivered from the Israelite attack on the city of Jericho.

Rahab agrees to the demands of the spies. She sends them on their way to hide in the hill country, and then she immediately ties the sign of the covenant in her window. This prompt action reflects the conviction, courage and obedience of Rahab.

The spies return to Joshua (2:22–24)

The two spies listen to Rahab's advice, and they flee to the highlands for three days. The soldiers of Jericho search diligently, literally, 'in every way', or 'on every road', but they are unable to capture the Israelite spies. Rahab once again protects the spies. The Lord's provision often comes in such strange and unconventional ways—one would have thought that the Lord would have protected these men with armies, or even angels, but by the hand of a prostitute? That God works in this way, however, magnifies his name, underscores his work and demonstrates his matchless love and mercy.

The spies go directly to Joshua. Using the exclamatory particle 'truly', or 'indeed', they tell him that the land is ripe for the picking. In fact, the men almost directly quote the words that

Rahab had said to them in verse 9. Their assessment of the land is exactly the opposite of that of the spies that Moses had sent earlier to look at the land, as recorded in Numbers 13:26–33. Those earlier spies concluded that Canaan is a land that is warlike and filled with people of such a great size that they are 'like grasshoppers' in their sight (Numbers 13:33). The spies sent out by Joshua are convinced that the land has been given to Israel by the Lord, and that its inhabitants have already 'melted before us'.[7]

Points to ponder

1. The providence of God in salvation
Rahab is a most unlikely Israelite ally. She is a pagan, a Canaanite, a female and a prostitute. But, of course, God is not bound by such things; he can change the heart of any person if he so wills it and desires it. His will and power work in the conversion of any life. The mysterious providence of God affects the salvation of sinners and the provision and protection of his own people.

The Metropolitan Tabernacle in London, where Charles Spurgeon pastored, was at one time undergoing massive renovation. So, during the week, many workmen laboured in the church. Spurgeon had the habit of going into his pulpit during the week to practise his sermon for the coming Sunday. One day he went out to practise his sermon and, paying no attention to all the activity and banging of the workmen, he went ahead and delivered his sermon. At the close of the practice message, a number of workmen came down from the scaffolding as believers, having been converted by hearing the Word of God preached. Oh, the mysterious providence of God in the salvation of sinners!

2. God can raise up people in the most unlikely situations

It needs to be noted that even in Jericho God has his people. When Paul and Barnabas were in Lystra they said to the people, 'In past generations he allowed all the nations to walk in their own ways. Yet he did not leave himself without witness ...' (Acts 14:16–17). Indeed, how often we see God raising up his people in the most unlikely times and places! John Craig, a Dominican friar who spent a number of years in a monastery in England, went to serve in a monastery in Bologna, Italy. One day, as he was in the monastery library, he came across a copy of Calvin's *Institutes of the Christian Religion*. He read it and was converted to the doctrines of grace. When Craig returned to Britain, he became a ministerial colleague of John Knox. Later he was the minister to King James (1580–1600). Does one not wonder how Calvin's *Institutes* made it into a Dominican monastery? God's hand can reach anyone at any time at any place.

3. Faith in action

Rahab's conversion is not merely a matter of belief, but confirmation of her faith attested by her works. James writes that '... in the same way was not also Rahab the prostitute justified by works when she received the messengers and sent them out by another way? For as the body apart from the spirit is dead, so also faith apart from works is dead' (James 2:25–26). Rahab's true faith finds its expression in her helping to hide the men of Israel, men who were soldiers of Yahweh. She greatly risked her well-being as she took a stand for the God of Israel.

Throughout the history of the church Christians have often been called to take a stand for God at the risk and peril of their own lives. In 1662, the Great Ejectment, or Ejection, took place in Britain. Pastors who would not conform to the standards of the Church of England were dismissed from their pulpits, thrown out of their manses and cut off from their stipends. Over 400 men were ejected at this time, and many of them were forced to live off the land. Three years later a deadly plague engulfed the city of London. Thomas Vincent, in his book *God's Terrible Voice in the City*, describes how thousands of Londoners died that year from the sickness:

> Now the cloud is very black, and the storm comes down upon us very sharp. Now Death rides triumphantly on his pale horse through our streets; and breaks into every house almost, where any inhabitants are to be found. Now people fall as thick as leaves from the trees in autumn, when they are shaken by a mighty wind... Now in some places where the people did generally stay, not one house in a hundred but is infected; and in many houses half the family is swept away; in some the whole, from the eldest to the youngest; few escape with the death of but one or two; never did so many husbands and wives die together; never did so many parents carry their children with them to the grave...[8]

This was a dark and terrible time for London. Yet, it was not all bleak and grim. Although numerous ministers who had conformed to the Church of England fled the plague of London, Vincent tells of faithful, gospel-preaching ministers who came to London to serve the people. Many of these men were the ones who had been thrown out of their churches during the Great Ejectment. Vincent remarks, 'Now they are preaching, and every sermon was unto them, as if they were preaching their last.'[9] The response was electrifying as many people were brought to a saving knowledge of Jesus Christ through God's mercy and grace. But why did these ministers, safely dwelling in the countryside, return to the city and risk death? Because they were men of faith, did not fear death and saw London as an opportunity to serve Christ and to take a stand for him.

4

Dividing of the Jordan River

Please read Joshua 3:1–17

One of the great themes of the Bible is God's creation and preparation of a good and pleasant land for his creatures, particularly humanity, to inhabit. In Genesis 1:6–10, God divides the waters, brings forth 'dry land', and then graciously and abundantly supplies resources for the needs of his people. The Hebrew word for 'dry land' means 'dry/withered/ without moisture/drained'.[1] It is often used of very dry ground as opposed to the waters of the sea. God simply brings forth the dry ground upon which his land creatures might live and flourish.

This pattern of water separation and land preparation is repeated in the book of Exodus in the Red Sea episode. In Exodus 14:15–16 we read, 'The LORD said to Moses, "Why do you cry to me? Tell the people of Israel to go forward. Lift up your staff, and stretch out your hand over the sea and divide it, that the people of Israel may go through the sea on dry ground."' The final word of the text is the same word as 'dry land' in Genesis 1:9. When the nation of Israel faces the Red Sea, God divides the waters of chaos, thereby opening the way for his people to move forward. Then he leads them to a new land where he sufficiently supplies all their needs.

This pattern appears a third time in Scripture in the historical events of Joshua 3–4. In this account, God divides the waters of the Jordan River, brings his people through the waters on 'dry ground' (4:22) and beneficently supplies them with a land flowing with milk and honey. In one sense, the episode is a re-creation account: God has prepared a new habitation for his people, a veritable Garden of Eden (Ezekiel 36:35; Joel 2:3).

To the Jordan River (3:1–6)

The Israelites have been encamped at the site of Shittim, approximately seven miles east of the Jordan River. Now they journey and make camp on the eastern bank of that river. At the close of a three-day bivouac, the military officers[2] pass through the Israelite camp to deliver a message to all the people. The core of the message is simple: when the people see the ark of the covenant being carried by the Levites, then they are to break camp and follow the ark. The laws of the Torah dictate that the Levites carry the ark. According to Numbers 4, the Kohathite clan of the tribe of Levi 'are to carry' (Numbers 4:15) the ark of the covenant by poles inserted in its sides (Numbers 4:5–6). The one caveat given in the command for Israel to follow the ark is that the people are to maintain a distance of 2,000 cubits to the rear of the ark. This measurement equals 3,000 feet (or just over 900 metres), well over half a mile in distance.

God gave the ark of the covenant as the central symbol of his presence with Israel in the wilderness, and it led them to the very edge of the promised land. Now it will lead the Israelites across the Jordan River into the land of Canaan. Therefore, not only has God granted Israel possession of the land (Deuteronomy 31:23; Joshua 1:6), but he is leading them and going before them into the land (Deuteronomy 31:3). The reality is that Israel does not know where to go, and so they must stand back and watch, and follow where God leads them. This should serve as encouragement for the people of God; the very presence and leadership of God ought to embolden and comfort them as they face squarely the prospects of war. This is true for the people of God throughout the ages.

> Sometimes 'mid scenes of deepest gloom,
> Sometimes where Eden's bowers bloom,
> By waters calm, o'er troubled sea,
> Still 'tis his hand that leadeth me.
> He leadeth me, he leadeth me;
> By his own hand he leadeth me;
> His faithful foll'wer I would be,
> For by his hand he leadeth me.   (Joseph Gilmore, 1862)

Now Joshua steps in and commands all the Israelites to 'consecrate yourselves', using an imperative. The basic meaning of this verb is 'to make holy', which bears the idea of setting something apart as distinct and wholly other; it is to set something apart from the unclean, thus purifying it. The text does not tell us how the Israelites are to consecrate themselves. However, Exodus 19 may give us some insight—in that passage the Israelites are commanded to consecrate themselves (v. 10) before they come to Mount Sinai, and this involves the washing of all their garments (v. 10) and abstention from sexual relations (v. 15).

The reason the Israelites are to purify themselves is expressly stated: the next day they will see God perform 'wonders' in their midst. 'Wonders' is a word commonly used to describe Israel's escape from Egypt and, in particular, the marvellous acts that God performed there—the plagues and the dividing of the Red Sea (Exodus 11:9; 15:11). Is Israel, therefore, to expect similar divine activity?

Joshua then commands the priests to carry the ark in front of the people, and they obey.

The command to cross the Jordan (3:7–13)

Perhaps the greatest, or at least the most dramatic, act that God performed by the hand of Moses was the dividing of the Red Sea (Exodus 14). Later Old Testament writers acknowledge this fact (see Isaiah 63:11-12; Psalm 74:13; 78:13; 106:9; 114:3). Now God is about to do a similar act at the Jordan River under the covenantal leadership of Joshua. One of the primary reasons for this divine action is so that all Israel will know that, as God 'was with Moses', so he will be with Joshua (3:7).

God orders Joshua to command the priests to go to the Jordan River, walk into it and take up a standing position in the water (3:8). Joshua then summons the people to hear the very word of God (3:9). He encourages the Israelites by telling them that the divine act they are about to witness is evidence that God is indeed with them and leading them. It will demonstrate that Yahweh is a 'living God'; this is a rare epithet for God in the Old Testament (see Psalm 42:2; 84:2; Hosea 1:10). It signifies that Yahweh is a God of being and doing; he truly exists and he acts in and through creation. And, moreover, he works particularly on behalf of his people. He is unlike idols that are mere metal, wood, or stone—they are truly inanimate, lifeless and inactive (see Psalm 115:3–8).

The divine act of dividing the waters of the Jordan also demonstrates that God 'will without fail drive out' the inhabitants of the land of Canaan. The verb here is a double verb in the original Hebrew: it literally reads, 'driving out, he will drive out'—this accentuates the claim being made. Seven people groups are listed as inhabitants of the land of Canaan. Such a list appears ten times in the Pentateuch. The listings, however, differ in the number of nations included. Genesis 15:18–21 includes ten nations, although most of the biblical lists mention fewer than seven.[3] Perhaps the seven nations listed in the present text symbolize totality and completion. Thus Joshua is declaring that God will dispossess all the people who are currently living in the land without exception.

Twice in the last three verses of this section (3:11,13) Joshua calls Yahweh 'the Lord of all the earth'. He uses this name to inspire confidence in the Israelites: not only are the waters of the Jordan River under his control and purview, but he is master of the entire planet! Who can stand against him?

Joshua tells the people what is about to happen. When the priests who carry the ark of the covenant stand still in the waters of the Jordan, then the waters that flow from the north will be cut off. In fact, the waters 'shall stand in one heap'. This language is employed elsewhere in the Old Testament, particularly of the dividing of the Red Sea. In Exodus 15:8, Moses exalts the Lord at the sea by saying:

At the blast of your nostrils the waters piled up;

the floods stood up in a pile [or 'heap'];
the deeps congealed in the heart of the sea.

The psalmist similarly proclaims, 'He divided the sea and let them pass through it, and made the waters stand like a heap' (Psalm 78:13). The language is also used of the activity of God in creation: 'He gathers the waters of the sea as a heap; he puts the deeps in storehouses' (Psalm 33:7). The dividing of the Jordan River is a wondrous re-creation event in which God brings forth the dry ground by splitting the waters, and then he takes his people through the waters and plants them in the promised land.

In verse 12, Joshua commands the people to choose one man from each of the twelve tribes. He states no purpose for this election. The reason is given later in the story, beginning in chapter 4:1.

Standing in a heap (3:14–17)

The event of the dividing of the Jordan River occurs exactly as Joshua had described it in verses 9–13. The people of Israel strike camp and they follow at a distance the Levitical priests who are bearing the ark of the covenant. As soon as the feet of the priests touch the water of the Jordan at its very edge, the waters divide and stand as a heap. At certain times of the year, the Jordan River is not very wide or very deep. However, the biblical writer tells us that during the time of harvest the Jordan River is inundated and its banks are overflowing. The Hebrew term for 'harvest' principally refers to the harvest of grain, such as wheat and barley, which occurs in Canaan in the late months of spring. The biblical author includes this aside so that the reader will allow no naturalistic explanation for the crossing of the Jordan. The people did not wade across a low Jordan—not so; only God's miraculous intervention allowed Israel to cross the deep and wide Jordan on dry ground.

The waters stand still and rise up in a heap at the site of Adam, a great distance from where the Israelites are crossing. Adam is a settlement that lies immediately next to the Jordan River on its eastern bank, approximately *sixteen miles* north of Jericho. This is the only time an Old Testament writer mentions this town, which is no doubt why he further explains that it lies near the better-known city of Zarethan (see Judges 7:22; 1 Kings 4:12; 7:46). Zarethan lies approximately *eighteen miles* north of Jericho. The point here is that the division of the Jordan River and the bringing forth of dry land is not a small thing—the separation is at least sixteen miles wide, and perhaps even wider, since the river also dried up from Jericho south to the Dead Sea (see 3:16). The latter distance is at least another five miles. Such a wondrous and spectacular event can be nothing less than the very hand of God!

While the people of Israel cross on 'dry ground', the priests who are bearing the ark stand 'firmly on dry ground' in the midst of the river. The term 'dry ground', used twice in verse 17, is a different word from that for 'dry land' discussed at the beginning of this chapter. However, it is also used with reference to the dividing of the Red Sea (see Exodus 14:21). Once again, the parting of the waters during the Exodus serves as a paradigm, or model, for the parting of the waters at the Jordan River.

Points to ponder

1. The inheritance God is preparing for his people
The re-creation pattern that begins at the creation, repeats at the Red Sea and is repeated again at the Jordan River consists

of God dividing waters, preparing a land and placing his people on that land. This theme is further developed in the New Testament, where it is directly applied to the church. In 1 Peter 1:3–4, the apostle tells the church:

> Blessed be the God and Father of our Lord Jesus Christ! According to his great mercy, he has caused us to be born again to a living hope through the resurrection of Jesus Christ from the dead, to an inheritance that is imperishable, undefiled, and unfading, kept in heaven for you.

The Septuagint, a Greek translation of the Old Testament, uses the word 'inheritance' for the land of promise—that is, the land of Canaan that Israel inherited. Through the work of Christ, God has prepared a land inheritance for the true church that will never perish, never fade and never be defiled. Heaven is an eternal land into which God is leading and placing his people.

The author of the book of Hebrews presents a similar idea. He says, 'For here we have no lasting city, but we seek the city that is to come' (Hebrews 13:14). As the people of God, Christians are not seeking for an earthly city. We are looking for an eternal city in an eternal land with eternal foundations! We seek the New Jerusalem, the holy city, 'coming down out of heaven from God' (Revelation 21:10).

Church hymnody often gives expression to this biblical theme as it applies to the church. The third stanza of the well-known hymn by William Williams says of the believer's pilgrimage:

> When I tread the verge of Jordan,
> bid my anxious fears subside;
> death of death, and hell's destruction,

land me safe on Canaan's side.

('Guide Me, O Thou Great Jehovah', 1745)

2. Crossing the river

John Bunyan's allegory *The Pilgrim's Progress* pictures two characters, Christian and Hopeful, at the end of their journey to the eternal inheritance. They are about to cross the river in order to enter the gates of the eternal city of Jerusalem. Bunyan relates the episode as follows:

They then addressed themselves to the water; and entering, Christian began to sink, and crying out to his good friend Hopeful, he said, 'I sink in deep waters; the billows go over my head, all his waves go over me!' ...

Then said the other, 'Be of good cheer, my brother, I feel the bottom, and it is good.' Then said Christian, 'Ah! ... I shall not see the land that floweth with milk and honey'; and with that a great darkness and horror fell upon Christian, so that he could not see before him. Also here he in a great measure lost his senses, so that he could neither remember nor orderly talk of any of those sweet refreshments that he had met with in the way of his pilgrimage. But all the words that he spake still tended to discover that he had horror of mind, and heart fears that he should die in that river, and never obtain entrance in at the gate. Here also, as they that stood by perceived, he was much in the troublesome thoughts of the sins that he had committed, both since and before he began to be a pilgrim. It was also observed that he was troubled with apparitions of hobgoblins and evil spirits, for ever and anon he would intimate so much by words.

Hopeful, therefore, here had much ado to keep his brother's head above the water; yea, sometimes he would be quite gone down, and then, ere a while, he would rise up again half dead. Hopeful also would endeavour to comfort him, saying, 'Brother, I see the gate, and men standing by to receive us'; but Christian would answer, 'It is you, it is you they wait for; you have been hopeful ever since I knew you.' 'And so have you,' said he to Christian. 'Ah! brother!' said he, 'surely if I was right he would now arise to help me: but for my sins he hath brought me into the snare, and hath left me.' Then said Hopeful, 'My brother, you have quite forgot the text, where it is said of the wicked, "There are no bands in their death, but their strength is firm. They are not troubled as other men, neither are they plagued like other men." These troubles and distresses that you go through in these waters are no sign that God hath forsaken you; but are sent to try you, whether you will call to mind that which heretofore you have received of his goodness, and live upon him in your distresses.'

Then I saw in my dream [says Bunyan], that Christian was as in a muse a while. To whom also Hopeful added this word, 'Be of good cheer, Jesus Christ maketh thee whole.' And with that Christian brake out with a loud voice, 'Oh, I see him again! And he tells me, "When thou passest through the waters, I will be with thee; and through the rivers, they shall not overflow thee."'

The eighteenth-century hymn 'How Firm a Foundation' summarizes this truth well when it says:

When through the deep waters I call you to go,
the rivers of sorrow shall not overflow;

For I will be with you, your troubles to bless,
and sanctify to you your deepest distress.

5

Standing stones

Please read Joshua 4:1–10

Often in the Old Testament men erected memorials to commemorate great events, especially direct meetings with Almighty God. For example, Genesis 28:10–22 records an episode involving a dream sequence in which Jacob has an encounter with the Lord. Following that meeting, Jacob takes the stone upon which his head had been resting and he sets it up as a stone of commemoration.

The purpose of a memorial, however, is more than mere commemoration for the individuals who erect the monuments; memorials are also for future generations to bring to mind past experiences in such a way that the remembrance affects present feeling, thought and action. In response to Korah's rebellion in Numbers 16, the Lord commanded Eleazar the priest to take the bronze censers of the rebels and hammer them into a covering for the altar of the tabernacle, 'to be a reminder to the people of Israel, so that no outsider, who is not of the descendants of Aaron, should draw near to burn incense before the LORD' (Numbers 16:39–40).

Memorials are a sub-category of symbolism. In Scripture, a symbol may be defined as a physical sign that represents a spiritual reality. In other words, a symbol is a visual representation of an invisible reality. So, for example, the Hebrew word for 'sign' or 'symbol' is used in Genesis 9:12–13, which says, 'And God said, "This is the sign of the covenant that I make between me and you and every living creature that is with you, for all future generations: I have set my bow in the cloud, and it shall be a sign of the covenant between me and the earth."' The rainbow is a physical sign of a spiritual reality—that is, the covenantal relationship between God and the earth. The rainbow is not the covenant, but it is a physical pointer to it. In like manner, circumcision serves as a symbol, or sign, in the Old Testament: 'You shall be circumcised in the flesh of your foreskins, and it shall be a sign of the covenant between me and you' (Genesis 17:11).

In the present episode in Joshua, the Hebrew term for 'sign' or 'symbol' is used to describe the construction of a signpost (4:6). It is a memorial that points to a grand spiritual reality and truth.

Picking up rocks (4:1–4)
The Lord orders Joshua to select twelve men (cf. 3:12), one from each tribe, and to tell them each to lift a stone out of the Jordan River. The stones are not to be taken from just anywhere in the river, but from the exact spot where the priests are standing who are carrying the ark of the covenant. Taking the stones from there is probably symbolic of God's presence with his people.

The stones are to remind Israel of his infinite power and his presence dwelling with them.

Stone memorials are extant in ancient Near-Eastern contexts. For instance, at the site of Gezer, archaeologists discovered a complex consisting of ten standing stones, none of which had been dressed. They were lined up in a straight north-south direction. The installation dates to around 1650 BC, prior to Israel's entrance into the land of promise. The excavator, R. A. S. Macalister, thought the structure was a series of stones that represented various deities protecting the Canaanite city of Gezer. In reality, the Gezer shrine perhaps commemorates the uniting of ten Canaanite groups or tribes into a covenant agreement with one another and with some deities.

There is an interesting wordplay in the text regarding the twelve men who were chosen. In verse 3, the priests carrying the ark are described as standing 'firmly' in the Jordan River. The next verse (4:4) then describes the twelve men whom Joshua called out of the tribes: they are those 'whom he had appointed'. The verb translated 'to appoint' is the same one as in verse 3; the text literally says, 'whom he had made firm' from among the sons of Israel. These twelve men are not ones who have merely been selected and appointed, but they are men who are instilled with steadfast, immoveable and firm character.

The Lord then tells Joshua to command the men to take the stones out of the Jordan and carry them to the place where Israel will camp in the land of Canaan.

The significance of the rocks (4:5–7)
The symbolic nature of the stones has a didactic purpose. And it is not merely for the present generation that is crossing the

Jordan River; it is for their posterity as well. This is evident in verse 6, in which the writer explicitly says that the Israelites' children will see the stones set up at the Jordan, and they will ask their parents, 'What do those stones mean to you?' The children will be curious about the stones. The purpose must be explained to them. A similar incident occurs at the first Passover; Moses tells the people that in the days to come their children will ask, 'What do you mean by this service?' (Exodus 12:26). The parental duty is to spell out clearly the meaning of the symbols of Passover. It is to have an illuminating and didactic effect: God is real, and he acts within history and on behalf of his people. They must remember.

The answer to the children's question is found in Joshua 4:7. The stones symbolize that when the ark of the covenant, itself a representation of the very presence of God, went into the Jordan, then the waters of the river separated. They testify to the power and presence of God with his people—in reality, they give a mere glimpse of the work of the Almighty on behalf of his people. What great encouragement to all the people of God as they are about to clash with formidable enemies in the land of Canaan! The work of God in separating the waters of the Jordan is the main point of the stones, and this is confirmed by repetition in verse 7:

a	b	c
The waters of the Jordan	were cut off	before the ark of the covenant
c^1	a^1	b^1
when it crossed	the waters of the Jordan	were cut off

The stones are called a 'memorial' for Israel 'for ever'. The most common sense of the word 'memorial' in Scripture is that of a monument that reminds one of something else. For example, in Exodus 28:12,29, the high priest is to wear an ephod and a breastpiece that bear twelve gems as a 'remembrance', or 'memorial', that he represents the twelve tribes of Israel before God. In like manner, the twelve stones of the Jordan are a monument to remind Israel of God's presence with them and his great power that divided the river in two.

Verse 7 states that 'these stones shall be to the people of Israel a memorial for ever'. There is no evidence that the twelve stones are standing at the river today, so in what sense is there an eternal element to the memorial? How can this be true? It is important for us to understand that the Scriptures teach that the recording of an event in writing can serve as a 'memorial' to future generations. Thus, for example, in Exodus 17:14, when God deals with the pagan Amalekites, he tells Moses to 'Write this as a memorial in a book and recite it in the ears of Joshua, that I will utterly blot out the memory of Amalek from under heaven.' The book itself is a physical object and a reminder of a divine promise. The recording of the establishment of the twelve stones in the Jordan River in Scripture is a memorial. And the Scriptures, which 'will stand for ever' (Isaiah 40:8), have an eternal application to the people of God.

Obedience (4:8–10)

The Israelites obey the orders of Joshua. The text uses a common linguistic formula from the Old Testament which indicates that the people did exactly what Joshua had commanded (4:8; cf. Exodus 39:1,5,26,43, etc.). The twelve men lifted twelve stones out of the river where the priests stood with the ark, and they took the stones to the camp of Israel on the west side of the Jordan River.

In verse 9, the text tells us that Joshua then had twelve other stones 'set up' in the very spot where the priests stood bearing the ark. This verb in Hebrew often means 'to stand up', which is the idea being conveyed. The stones are standing pillars that can be seen, and they attest to the standing covenant relationship between God and Israel. And they are, moreover, a lasting sign of God's great and powerful act at the Jordan River.

The author of the book adds an editorial comment when he says that the stones 'are there to this day' (4:9). We are uncertain who the author is, and so we are also uncertain of the historical context of the time in which he is writing. His point, however, is well taken: the monument is not failing in its purpose. The stones are yet standing at a later date as a symbol and sign of God's work; they have not been knocked down or washed away. They indeed have a lasting and abiding significance.

Points to ponder

Signs and symbols in the life of the church

The church employs signs and symbols in its life and worship. The sacraments, baptism and the Lord's Supper, are defined by the *Westminster Confession of Faith* as 'holy signs and seals of the covenant of grace, immediately instituted by God, to represent Christ, and His benefits' (Ch. XXVII:1). In other words, the sacraments are, on one level, physical signs and pointers to covenantal, spiritual truths.

Sacraments, like signs in the Old Testament, have past, present and future applications. Thus, for example, communion reflects a past reality as a sign and symbol of Christ's death on the cross: 'This is my body, which is given for you' (Luke 22:19). It also has a present relevance to those taking communion to remind them of their covenant responsibilities: 'This is my blood of the covenant' (Mark 14:24). In addition, the Lord's Supper points to the anticipated future return of Christ: 'For as often as you eat this bread and drink the cup, you proclaim the Lord's death until he comes' (1 Corinthians 11:26). The sacraments are also similar to symbols in the Old Testament because they apply not only to one generation, but to the entire church in perpetuity. The various meanings of the sacraments apply to one church generation after another.

The final act at the Jordan River

Please read Joshua 4:11–24

In one sense believers are called to live fearlessly. During the so-called 'sifting times' in seventeenth-century Scotland, many believers were called to face persecution, and even death, without fear. As two believers stood on the scaffold ready to die, one Covenanter said to the other, 'Brother, die well, it is the last act of faith you will ever be able to do.' In another episode, two Covenanter pastors stood at the bottom of the steps that led to the scaffold and their execution. One turned to the other and said, 'I have less fear climbing these steps than the steps of the pulpit.' Believers, indeed, are to be firm, resolved, steadfast, and to bring glory to God, no matter what their circumstances, even unto death. May our prayer at the trial of death be: 'O Lord, let me die well and let me die bringing glory and honour to your name.' Fearless!

Does this mean believers are never to fear? Is fear always

to be shunned, fought against and conquered? Is fear merely a negative concept, then? No, indeed; when it is understood properly and applied appropriately, fear is a good thing. In the Old Testament, the Hebrew verb 'to fear' appears over four hundred times, and in almost eighty per cent of those occurrences the object of fear is God. The verb carries the general sense of the awe of God that leads to obedience and to worship of him. This type of fear is good and necessary. In the book of Deuteronomy, Moses posed the following salient question to Israel:

> And now, Israel, what does the LORD your God require of you, but to fear the LORD your God, to walk in all his ways, to love him, to serve the LORD your God with all your heart and with all your soul, and to keep the commandments and statutes of the LORD, which I am commanding you today for your good? (Deuteronomy 10:12–13).

Truly, the 'fear of the LORD is the beginning of knowledge' (Proverbs 1:7).

In the opening chapters of the book of Joshua, the Israelites, from a human perspective, have every reason to be afraid. They have lost their leader, Moses; they are facing the obstacle of an inundated Jordan River; and they are about to confront militarily the peoples of the land of Canaan, who are formidable opponents. Yet God tells the Israelites not to fear, but rather to 'be strong and very courageous' (1:6,7,9). They are to bear up to these adverse circumstances fearlessly. Conversely, at the very close of the present passage, Joshua tells all Israel that they ought to 'fear the LORD your God for ever' (4:24). They are to have a righteous, reverent fear, and one that is directed towards Yahweh, the God of Israel.

Prepared for battle (4:11–13)

This passage adds to the description of Israel's crossing of the Jordan River. It relates how 40,000 men, 'ready', or 'equipped', 'for war', cross first into the land of Canaan. This wing of the Israelite army crosses 'before the people of Israel' (4:12) and 'before the Lord'—that is, before the ark of the covenant leaves the riverbed (4:11). This battle-group is comprised of soldiers from the tribes of Reuben, Gad and the half-tribe of Manasseh. Moses had made these tribes swear that their soldiers would be the first to penetrate Canaan, 'to go before the people of Israel' (Numbers 32:17; cf. Joshua 1:14). These tribes keep the vow that they had made.

The troops cross the Jordan River, literally, 'in battle array'. This is exactly the same wording that was used of Israel when the people came forth out of the land of Egypt during the Exodus (see Exodus 13:18). The Israelites left a land of hostility 'in battle array', and now they are entering a land of hostility in the same manner.

Elevation of Joshua (4:14)

On the day that Israel crosses the Jordan River, the Lord, literally, 'caused Joshua to be great' before the children of Israel. It is the Lord who exalts leaders and deposes them: 'He changes times and seasons; he removes kings and sets up kings' (Daniel 2:21; cf. Daniel 4:17); 'It is God who executes judgement, putting down one and lifting up another' (Psalm 75:7). The exaltation of Joshua is the fulfilment of God's promise to him in Joshua 3:7.

The text says that the people, literally, 'feared' Joshua as they had 'feared' Moses. This is a good type of fear that is to be understood as awe and respect towards the covenant mediator. Israel is not to 'fear' the Canaanites (Deuteronomy 31:6–7), but they are to be strong and courageous before them. On the other hand, they are to have a healthy 'fear' of God (4:24) and of his covenant mediator Joshua.

Returning of the waters (4:15–19)

After the leading military units and the remainder of the people following them pass over the Jordan, only then does God, through Joshua, order the priests who are carrying the ark to come up out of the riverbed. As soon as the priests' feet touch the dry ground on the western bank of the river, then the waters of the Jordan 'returned to their place', continue their flow and overrun the banks of the riverbed.

The regression of the river to its earlier state prior to God's intervention is reminiscent of the dividing of the Red Sea. After all the Israelites had crossed through the Red Sea, the text reads:

> Moses stretched out his hand over the sea, and the sea returned to its normal course when the morning appeared. And as the Egyptians fled into it, the LORD threw the Egyptians into the midst of the sea. The waters returned and covered the chariots and the horsemen; of all the host of Pharaoh that had followed them into the sea, not one of them remained (Exodus 14:27–28).

The verb 'returned', used twice in this passage, is the same one describing the regression of the waters of the Jordan River here in Joshua 4:18.

The receding of the waters at the moment that the priests step out of the water confirms that the entire event at the Jordan River was supernatural. The timing and work belong to Yahweh. It cannot be explained naturally, nor can it be dismissed as trickery, chicanery, or deception. God is working on behalf of his people—it is nothing less than that!

The biblical writer sets the event of the crossing into a temporal structure; he says that it is completed, and then that Israel encamps at Gilgal 'on the tenth day of the first month'. The latter is no random date; the book of Exodus tells us that this was the very day on which the first Passover began: 'This month shall be for you the beginning of months. It shall be the first month of the year for you. Tell all the congregation of Israel that on the tenth day of this month every man shall take a lamb according to their fathers' houses...' (Exodus 12:2–3). Thus, the Passover date in Exodus marks Israel's departure from the land of death and darkness (Egypt), and now in Joshua it marks their entrance into the land of promise and life (Canaan).

The precise location of Gilgal is uncertain. It is perhaps located at Khirbet el-Mafjar, a mound that sits approximately two miles north-east of Jericho.

Erection of standing stones at Gilgal (4:20–24)
Once the people encamp at Gilgal, Joshua has the twelve stones he had taken from the Jordan River set up. Then Joshua explains to the people the didactic nature of the monuments: the stones are to be instructive to future generations of Israelites. Children will ask their parents the meaning of the stones at Gilgal (cf. 4:6). The answer to their question is threefold.

First, the stones represent the historical incident in which the Lord 'dried up' the waters of the Jordan so that Israel could cross unharmed into the promised land. The verb for 'dried up' is a Hiphil in Hebrew, which is the causative stem. The idea is that God is the one at work in the dividing of the waters; he caused them to dry up. Thus, the monuments are representative of God's powerful work on behalf of his people.

Secondly, the monument has a missionary purpose. It declares to 'the earth' that 'the hand of the LORD [Yahweh] is mighty'. The separation of the Red Sea also proclaimed the power and glory of God to others. When Jethro, Moses' father-in-law, heard of the event at the Red Sea, he confessed, 'Now I know that the LORD is greater than all gods...' (Exodus 18:11). Rahab made a similar response earlier in the book of Joshua (2:10–11).

The final significance of the stones is so 'that you may fear the LORD your God for ever'. Both the subject pronoun ('you') and the possessive pronoun ('your') are second-person plurals, referring to the covenant people of Israel. Israel is not to 'fear' the enemies in the land of promise (see Deuteronomy 1:21; 20:3; 31:6), but they are to 'fear' Yahweh their God. This 'fear' is a good and proper one; it is an awe that the people are to have that will lead them to their obedience and worship of the one true God.

Points to ponder

1. Christians are not to fear the things of this world that may threaten them

W.S. Plumer put it this way: 'The righteous will not yield to disastrous fear, though the nations are convulsed with terrible excitements, and all the safeguards of society are gone.'

In response to one of William Cowper's most distressing and fearful times in a life racked with depression, John Newton wrote the following words to him:

But if he is the Captain of our salvation, if his eye is upon us, his arm stretched out around us, and his ear open to our cry, and if he has engaged to teach our hands to war and our fingers to fight, and to cover our heads in the day of battle, then we need not fear, though a host rise up against us; but, lifting up our banner in his name, let us go forth conquering and to conquer.

What do you fear? Are you afraid of death? Sickness? Pain? Separation? Can you define your true fears? A unique answer to those questions was once given by Chrysostom, the great Church Father. Empress Eudoxia had been sending him deeply threatening letters—against his very life. His response is illuminating: '*Nil nisi peccatum timeo.*' That Latin saying is simply translated as: 'I fear nothing but sin.' What do you fear?

2. A fearless Christian is not self-made and self-grown

We need to understand that a believer does not endure suffering, persecution and evil in and of himself. It is not 'Buck up,' or 'Have a stiff upper lip,' that gives courage and endurance to a Christian. Rather, bravery derives from the very presence of God. Calvin explained, 'If we desire to be protected by the hand of God, we must be concerned above all things that he may dwell amongst us; for all hope of safety depends on his presence alone.' 'The best of all,' said John Wesley at his death, 'is, God is with us.' It is only the presence of God that can provide true courage and fortitude in a believer to face the perils of the world and the darts of the devil.

A good example of this truth is found in Psalm 57, in which David is running for his life from the evil intentions and pursuit of Saul. He realizes that the 'storms of destruction' are passing over him (v. 1), and how does he respond? He calls out to God for mercy; he comes into God's presence and seeks the grace that will sustain him. This raises the question for each one of us: where do we flee in times of hostility? To whom do we go in times of trouble and hardship? Perhaps we begin with our spouse, or our parents, or a friend. And, indeed, these are people to go to for aid; however, they are mere people who themselves are weak, fragile and limited creatures. David rightly begins with the sovereign Lord of the universe, the providential God who sits enthroned over all. That is why David can conclude in the psalm that 'My heart is steadfast, O God, my heart is steadfast!' (v. 7).

3. The believer is not to be fearless in all things

The Scriptures are clear that Christians are to fear the Lord. We have already defined 'the fear of God' as an awe that leads to obedience and worship. This is where true godly knowledge, wisdom and living begin. And the consequence of the believer's fear of God is immense: 'A right fear of God is the antidote to every other fear.'[1] John Bunyan, who was constantly in circumstances that would evoke fear, commented:

> Remember what a world of privileges do belong to them that fear the Lord ... namely, that such shall not be hurt, shall want no good thing, shall be guarded by angels, and have a special licence, though in never so dreadful a plight, to trust in the name of the Lord, and stay upon their God.[2]

7

Setting one's house into proper spiritual order

Please read Joshua 5:1-12

I n the Old Testament perhaps the two most important signs or symbols that set Israel apart to the Lord are circumcision and the celebration of Passover. They are both physical signs of a spiritual reality (see the use of the word 'sign' in Genesis 17:11 and Exodus 12:13). And that spiritual reality is that Israel is in covenant relationship with the Lord; they indeed belong to him. Those two rituals, furthermore, are to be carried out 'throughout your generations' (Genesis 17:9,12; Exodus 12:14,17). It is important to observe that the first generation that came out of Egypt were circumcised and had celebrated the Passover twice, once in Egypt and once at Mount Sinai (Numbers 9:1-14). That generation, however, broke the covenant with the Lord and they were cursed by him to die in the wilderness. The second generation of Israelites were neither circumcised in the wilderness nor did they celebrate the Passover during that time. They did not bear the signs of being the covenant people of God until their entrance into the land of promise.

No lurking danger (5:1)

The leadership of the peoples of Canaan has no heart for confrontation with the Israelites. It is the 'kings of the Amorites' and the 'kings of the Canaanites' whose hearts have melted and who have no spirit for warfare. There is an ancient Arabic proverb that says, 'The fish stinks from the head,' and, indeed, if the kings have no stomach for a fight, then neither will their people. It is not that the pagan kings are afraid of the army of Israel. No, the text tells us that these leaders 'heard that the LORD [literally "Yahweh"] had dried up the waters of the Jordan'. They have a knee-knocking terror of the God of Israel.

The fact that the military threat to Israel is minimal at this time is important for what follows. Joshua, by the Lord's command, is about to circumcise all the adult males of Israel. The soldiers of Israel, therefore, will be incapacitated and disabled. They will, for a time, be unable to take up arms and defend the people (cf. Genesis 34:25–29).

Circumcision of the second generation (5:2–7)

In verse 2, God commands Joshua to go to the people and circumcise the adult males; the verb 'circumcise' is an imperative form. Joshua must obey the divine dictate. He is told to do this 'a second time'. To what does that refer? It probably relates to the fact that the first generation that came out of Egypt were all circumcised (see Exodus 12:43–51), but this 'second' generation do not bear that sign of the covenant (see 5:5).

Joshua obeys, and we see the renewal of the covenant sign on

Israel by the express command of God. This ritual takes place 'at Gibeath-haaraloth'. A direct translation of the Hebrew name of that site means 'unto the hill of foreskins'. Many commentators treat this as a proper name, and they argue that this was the hill's name prior to the circumcision of Israel. On the other hand, the name may simply be taken as descriptive of the massive circumcision event that had just taken place, and the name 'the hill of foreskins' may be derivative of the event.

Why had the second generation not been circumcised in the wilderness? The first generation broke the covenant, and the second generation did not receive the sign of the covenant. Perhaps the second generation had to bear the apostasy of their fathers until that former generation had been consumed in the wilderness. Thus, this 'second' circumcision represents a new beginning, and this is especially true because it is the second generation that will secure the land of promise.

One aspect of the covenant that is sealed by the sign of circumcision is that Israel would inherit 'a land flowing with milk and honey' (5:6). This is the only time that this epithet is used of the land of Canaan in the book of Joshua. Its use to describe Canaan is ironic. In Numbers 16:13, the Hebrews complain that Moses had brought them 'out of a land flowing with milk and honey', namely, Egypt. The fact is that Egypt was well known in antiquity for producing both of these commodities in abundance; it is an ironic twist that here these goods are attributed to the land of Canaan.

Revival (5:8–9)
After the national event of circumcision, the men remain in the camp 'until they were healed'. The verb 'to heal' in Hebrew derives from a basic form that means 'to live'. In one sense it

simply means that the men are recovering and reviving in the camp from their wounds. In another sense it signifies that the men are being brought to life as God's people in a new land.

The Lord then explains to Joshua the major consequence of the covenant act of circumcision that has just taken place. By it, God says that he has 'rolled away the reproach of Egypt'. The verb in that clause is commonly used in the Old Testament of someone rolling a stone away from the mouth of a well (Genesis 29:3,8) or a cave (see 10:18). God is simply removing an obstacle, and it is 'the reproach' of Egypt. What exactly that is referring to is difficult to know, although it may be related to the shame and disgrace that the Israelites incurred by being slaves in Egypt. Now they are free and are on the verge of securing their own land. The 'reproach of Egypt' may also refer to the taunts, jeers and general abuse that the Egyptians had heaped on the Israelites when in servitude. That abasement is all gone now; the Hebrews are in the land of promise and they bear the sign of their covenant relationship with the Lord. The Lord is their master, not the Egyptians!

Passover (5:10–12)

During the wilderness wanderings, the Israelites did not practise circumcision, a sign of the covenant. In like manner, there is no evidence that the Hebrews kept the Passover during their journeys from Egypt. Scripture describes the last Passover that Israel had celebrated; it was the second Passover celebration in the history of Israel and it took place at Mount Sinai (Numbers 9:1–14). They celebrated the Passover a year after God miraculously brought Israel out of the land of Egypt. God had abundantly provided for the people during that year, and he often did so using extraordinary means. At Sinai they celebrated the second Passover; it is a feast that recalls Israel's salvation and redemption from Egyptian slavery, or what Brown calls 'their unmerited deliverance'.[1] However, from the time at Sinai until Israel entered the land of Canaan, a span of approximately thirty-nine years, the feast of Passover was suspended and not kept by the people of God.

Now Israel celebrates its first Passover in the land of promise. This feast serves as an *inclusio* for the wilderness wanderings— that is, as bookends to the wanderings from Egypt to Canaan. It was observed on the day they left Egypt, and now it is performed in the first days that Israel is in the promised land. It is a sign for the people that they have indeed left the land of death and darkness, and now they have come into the land of life and light.

The day after the Passover service, the Israelites eat from the 'produce' of Canaan. This noun appears on only two occasions in the Hebrew language of the Old Testament, both of them in verses 11–12 of the present chapter. The word is related to the Hebrew verb 'to cross over', which is used so frequently in the early chapters of the book of Joshua (2:23; 3:1,4,16: 4:7,10,11,12,13,22,23). This is probably a wordplay that ties together Israel's 'crossing over' (Hebrew, *'br*) into Canaan with their eating of the 'produce' (Hebrew, *'br*) of the land.

The day after the people eat some of the produce of Canaan, the manna no longer rains down on them. The first provision of manna occurred prior to their arrival at Mount Sinai (Exodus 16), and that provision lasted in the wilderness for thirty-nine years. It was a wonderful, miraculous provision from God, although the Israelites often grumbled about it (Numbers 21:5). The manna, therefore, was a temporary provision for the people in their wanderings, but now in the land of promise they are eating the yield of their inheritance.

Points to ponder

1. Signs of the covenant

The Scots' Confession of 1560 makes the following proclamation regarding the sacraments of the church:

> As the fathers under the Law, besides the reality of the sacrifices, had two chief sacraments, that is, circumcision and the Passover, and those who rejected these were not reckoned among God's people; so do we acknowledge and confess that now in the time of the gospel we have two chief sacraments, which alone were instituted by the Lord Jesus and commanded to be used by all who will be counted members of his body, that is, Baptism and the Supper or Table of the Lord Jesus, also called the Communion of his body and blood. These sacraments, both of the Old Testament and of the New, were instituted by God not only to make a visible distinction between his people and those who were without the Covenant, but also to exercise the faith of his children and, by participation of these sacraments, to seal in their hearts the assurance of his promise, and of that most blessed conjunction, union, and society, which the chosen have with their Head, Christ Jesus (Chapter 21).

The Israelites are about to conquer the land of promise; however, before they attempt to seize the land they are to enact both Old Testament sacraments. These two rites are signs that Israel belongs to the Lord in covenant, and that the people of God are different from the peoples of the surrounding nations. Celebration of Passover and the rite of circumcision are witnesses to the fact that Israel has been set apart to the Lord out of all the peoples of the earth. In addition, these sacraments indicate that, as the people of God, the Israelites enjoy many blessings, and these include the inheritance of the land of promise and having been entrusted with the very oracles of God (Romans 3:1–2). The same truths apply to the church. When people are baptized into the church and regularly celebrate the Lord's Supper, they are demonstrating that they are part of the covenant community. They are in union with Christ, and they are part of his visible church. And, as members of the covenant community, they enjoy many blessings and benefits, such as fellowship with others in the covenant, hearing the Word of God preached and having the Bible.

2. Bread from heaven

The closing scene of this episode is that God ceases to rain down manna on the people. So ends a wonderful provision of the Lord to his people as they travelled through a barren, arid land. God blessed the people with manna almost as soon as they left Egypt (Exodus 16:15), and it continued to the point of their entrance into Canaan—that is, a forty-year period. Jesus uses the story of the manna as a teaching tool because it points to him and his work. In John 6, he says to the crowds at the Sea of Galilee:

> Do not labour for the food that perishes, but for the food that endures to eternal life... I say to you, it was not Moses who gave you the bread from heaven, but my Father gives you the true bread from heaven. For the bread of God is he who comes down from heaven and gives life to the world ... I am the bread that came down from heaven (John 6:27,32–33,41).

Yes, the provision of manna to the Israelites was a wonderful, miraculous provision of God, but something greater than manna has come. Jesus is the true bread that is not discontinued; he feeds his people unto eternal life. There is no cessation to the bread of Jesus, and so let us continue to feed upon him!

Part 2:

The seizing (5:13–12:24)

The fall of Jericho

Please read Joshua 5:13–6:27

In 1897, when George Müller was in his early nineties, he was interviewed and asked the following question: 'You have always found the Lord faithful to his promise?' Müller responded:

> Always. He has never failed me! For nearly seventy years every need in connection with this work has been supplied. The orphans, from the first until now, have numbered nine thousand five hundred, but they have never wanted a meal. Never! Hundreds of times we have commenced the day without a penny in hand, but our Heavenly Father has sent supplies by the moment they were actually required. There never was a time when there was no wholesome meal. During all these years I have been enabled to trust in God, in the living God, and in Him alone. One million four hundred thousand pounds have been sent to me in answer

to prayer. We have wanted as much as fifty thousand pounds in one year, and it has all come by the time it has been really needed.

In the present chapter we see God fulfilling his promises to his people by granting them entrance into the land of promise (Genesis 15:18; 24:7; 26:4; Numbers 34:2; Deuteronomy 34:4). The secondary, almost passive, role of Israel in capturing the city of Jericho is particularly striking in this narrative. God is fighting Israel's battle, and we need to recognize and acknowledge the centrality of his presence and activity in the conquest.

How will God act to fulfil his promise that Israel will inherit the land of Canaan? The answer to this question is quite surprising.

The commander of the Lord's army (5:13–15)

While the Israelites remain encamped at Gilgal, the text says that Joshua was 'by', or 'near', 'Jericho'. Why Joshua is there is not explicitly stated, although it is safe to assume that he is on a reconnaissance mission to scout Jericho in preparation for a battle.

As he surveys the area, Joshua sees 'a man' in front of him in a military stance. Who is this man? Although the figure is called 'a man' in the text, it is important to consider that this language does not necessarily mean that he is a human being. For example, in Genesis 18:2 three 'men' visit Abraham at the door of his tent; the text later explains that this was an appearance of the Lord and two of his angels. In Genesis 32, Jacob wrestles with 'a man' at the Jabbok River; speaking of the encounter, Jacob says, 'I have seen God face to face' (Genesis 32:24,30).

Who is this man standing before Joshua? A clue comes from the description of the figure: 'his drawn sword in his hand'. This precise expression is used in Numbers 22:23 to describe the angel of the Lord as he stood in a military stance before Balaam on the road.

Who is this man whom Joshua sees? In verse 15 the man tells Joshua: 'Take off your sandals from your feet, for the place where you are standing is holy.' This charge to Joshua is, almost verbatim, the charge that God gave to Moses at the burning bush (Exodus 3:5). Moreover, the text describes the scene as follows: 'the angel of the LORD appeared to him in a flame of fire out of the midst of a bush' (Exodus 3:2).

Based on the two parallels from Numbers and Exodus, we may assume that the man in Joshua 5:13–15, described as 'the commander of the LORD's army', is the angel of the Lord. But who is the angel of the Lord? In Exodus 3:4, at the burning bush, the angel is identified with God and speaks as if he is God. The Old Testament elsewhere indicates that the angel of the Lord is God (see Judges 13:17–22). The same is true in Joshua 5:14; the appearance of the angel of the Lord evokes awe, submission and worship on the part of Joshua, because the angel is God. In addition, it is likely that the word of God spoken to Joshua beginning in 6:2 is from the lips of the angel of the Lord. Some commentators argue that the angel of the Lord is the Second Person of the Trinity, a pre-incarnate appearance of Christ. As John Calvin remarks, 'But let us enquire who this Angel was? ... The ancient teachers of the Church have rightly understood [it to be] the Eternal Son of God in respect to his office as Mediator.'[1]

Joshua initially responds to the appearance of the angel of the

Lord by asking him, 'Are you for us, or for our adversaries?' The figure does not answer Joshua's question directly, but says, 'Now I have come.' He arrives as a fulfilment of the promise previously given by God to the people of Israel:

> Behold, I send an angel before you to guard you on the way and to bring you to the place that I have prepared. Pay careful attention to him and obey his voice; do not rebel against him, for he will not pardon your transgression, for my name is in him.

> But if you carefully obey his voice and do all that I say, then I will be an enemy to your enemies and an adversary to your adversaries.

> When my angel goes before you ... (Exodus 23:20–23).

This promised angel has now come to lead Israel into the land, and he is sufficient to do it because he is 'the commander of the army of the LORD'. The Hebrew term for 'army' is used in the Old Testament over 250 times referring to the 'hosts' of God (see, for example, 2 Samuel 5:10; 1 Kings 19:10,14). This army includes all the angels of the Lord, as well as various elements of creation, such as the stars in the sky (Deuteronomy 4:19). Consequently, the angel of the Lord will lead Israel into the land of promise, supported by the very fullness of the heavenlies of the Lord!

A parenthesis (6:1)

Joshua 6:1 is a parenthetical remark that briefly shifts the account to the location of the enemy and away from the dialogue between the angel of the Lord and Joshua. The narrative will return to their conversation in 6:2. In 6:1 we read that Jericho is sealed tightly. The text literally says, 'Jericho was shut up and it was shut up'; the double use of the verb is emphatic to underscore that from a military vantage point Jericho is secure and seemingly impregnable. Yet, as A. W. Pink once wrote, 'Man's extremity is God's opportunity.' Although from a human and strategic perspective Jericho appears unassailable, the reality is that Israel has the Lord and his army fighting for them!

The command of the commander (6:2–5)

The angel of the Lord, the commander of the heavenly army, now gives battle instructions to Joshua. The first thing he says is: 'I have given Jericho into your hand.' The tense of the verb here is one of completed action; it is not I 'will' give Jericho to you, but I 'have' given it to you. The conquest of the city is a done deal!

The angel then lays out the plan of attack. The conquest of the city will take seven days. On the first six days a procession will march around the city once each day. The order of the procession is explicit: the fighting men will lead the way, followed by seven priests who each have a trumpet, and then the ark of the covenant, carried by Levites (6:6). Finally, there is a 'rearguard' of soldiers that follows behind the ark (6:9). According to Beale, this marching formation is reminiscent of Egyptian battle configurations.[2] When the people of Jericho see the Israelite procession circling their city, it is likely that they will recognize it as a military machine.

On the seventh day, the military procession is to circle the city seven times (6:4). The number 'seven' plays a leading role in the narrative: there are seven priests, seven trumpets, seven days and seven marches around the city. In Hebrew culture the number seven often symbolizes completion or is a mark of an accomplished task. A prime example lies in the completion of creation on the seventh day (Genesis 2:1–3). Here in Joshua, it is on the seventh day that the event reaches a crescendo: the wall of Jericho falls down and the Israelite soldiers enter the city (6:5; cf. 6:20).

According to the divine battle plan, after the wall of Jericho collapses the Israelite soldiers 'shall go up, everyone straight before him' (6:5). The verb translated 'go up' means 'to ascend, rise'; the city of Jericho is a *tell*, which is defined as a high mound consisting of debris from cities built one on top of another. As such, *tells* have a steep, sloping configuration. Therefore, for the Israelites to enter the city they must 'go up' the mound of Jericho and then rush through the broken-down wall of the city.

Days one through six (6:6–14)

The Israelites are encamped at Gilgal (5:10). There Joshua summons the priests and he sets in order the procession that is to march around Jericho. He gives the marching order just as he was told to do by the angel of the Lord: the soldiers are to lead, and they are followed by seven priests with seven trumpets, the ark of the covenant which is carried by the Levites and finally, a military rearguard. Israel immediately obeys the command of God given through Joshua (6:8).

Joshua calls for complete silence on the part of those forming the procession as they march around Jericho (6:10). He is insistent in this matter, employing a triple negative in the command. Joshua literally says to the marchers, 'Do *not* shout … Do *not* let your voice be heard … Do *not* let a word go out of your mouth.' The only sound that is to be made is the continual blowing of the trumpets by the priests.

The Israelites follow these procedures on days one to six. The text is clear in this regard when it says, 'So they did for six days' (6:14). This statement underscores the obedience of Israel to the commands of God through Joshua.

The seventh day (6:15–19)

On the first six days of the siege the Israelites marched around the city once each day. Now, on the seventh day, they march around the city seven times. Apparently the people march silently the first six times that they encircle the city on the seventh day, but on the seventh circuit the priests blow the trumpets and Joshua commands the people to 'Shout' (6:16). Matters are coming to a crescendo; the siege is reaching a climax. However, before the reader is told what the result of the climactic seventh lap is, a parenthesis appears in the text.

One would expect the text to move directly from verse 16 to verse 20. Instead, some instructions are inserted for the Israelite forces to carry out during the assault on the city. The interruption of the flow of the narrative by the insertion of these instructions demonstrates how important they are for the episode.

Joshua tells the people of Israel that Jericho, and everything in the city, is to be 'devoted to the LORD for destruction'. The Hebrew term for 'devote to destruction' is *cherem*, and it literally means 'to put something under a ban for utter annihilation'. It is a word used in connection with a number of cities that are attacked during the conquest: Ai (8:26), Makkedah (10:28) and Hazor (11:11). Usually such a ban means that all living things are to be killed (1 Samuel 15:3). The word *cherem* is holy-war terminology in which unholy things are destroyed as a kind of sacrifice to the Lord.

The concept of *cherem* is not exclusively Israelite. King Mesha uses the term in the Moabite Stone in relation to his defeat of Nebo, which belonged to Israel. He says, 'And Chemosh said to me, "Go, take Nebo from Israel!" So I went by night and fought against it and slaying all, seven thousand men, boys, women, girls and maidservants, for I had devoted them to destruction for [the god] Ashtar-Chemosh.'[3]

For many people the *cherem* constitutes one of the great ethical dilemmas in the Old Testament. They would argue that it is unworthy of God to be depicted as sanctioning and ordering the total destruction of the Canaanites at Jericho. How could a holy and loving God give instructions for the utter annihilation of the Canaanites? This is a question of theodicy, which is an attempt to understand the nature and actions of God in the face of evil and suffering.[4] Again, how could God act this way?

A foundational observation to make is that God does, in fact, order the *cherem*. There is no way around this truth. Moses tells the people before the conquest:

> But in the cities of these peoples that the LORD your God is giving you for an inheritance, you shall save alive nothing that breathes, but you shall devote them to complete destruction [*cherem*], the Hittites and the Amorites, the Canaanites and the Perizzites, the Hivites and the Jebusites, as the LORD your God has commanded (Deuteronomy 20:16–17; cf. Deuteronomy 7:1–2).

How could God order such a thing? First, it needs to be pointed out that Israel is to take possession of the land by the immediate hand of God, *who has an absolute right to exercise his power in any way he wills.* It is God's desire, pleasure and purpose for Israel to inherit Canaan. When the apostle Paul explains the sovereignty of God to the men of Athens he includes the following description: 'And he made from one man every nation of mankind to live on all the face of the earth, having determined allotted periods and the boundaries of their dwelling place ...' (Acts 17:26).

Secondly, *the Canaanites were in no respect innocent* as they stood before God and Israel. Were they a peaceful, righteous, upright people? Were they in some way undeserving of God's justice? When God promised Abraham that his descendants would inherit the land of Canaan, he said it would not occur until 'the fourth generation' because 'the iniquity of the Amorites is not yet complete' (Genesis 15:16). Since the time of Abraham the Canaanites have been heaping up sin. Leviticus 18 recounts the wicked behaviour of the Canaanites: they practise child sacrifice, incest, adultery, temple prostitution and various other abominations. Therefore, we see God's justice going forth against the Canaanites in the book of Joshua because they rejected God and his law.

Israel acts as an instrument of God's judgement on the Canaanites. In one sense this should not be troubling since elsewhere God uses pagan nations to punish his own chosen people (Habakkuk 1:5-11; Isaiah 10). Why would he not employ the elect nation as a means of judgement on ungodly peoples? The Lord employs secondary causes in judgement, such as fire against Sodom and Gomorrah, or rain against the people in Noah's day. At Jericho, God simply uses Israel as his instrument of justice.

The *cherem* also serves the purpose of *God protecting his own people*. In Deuteronomy 20:18 the Lord provides the following reason that Israel is to destroy the many nations before them: '... that they may not teach you to do according to all their abominable practices that they have done for their gods, and so you sin against the LORD your God.' To put it simply, cohabitation with pagan nations in the land of promise makes Israel vulnerable to fall into wickedness.

There is an exception to all the human destruction that is to take place at Jericho. Rahab and her family 'shall live'; they shall be spared 'because she hid the messengers' (6:17). Rahab had acted in faith, and therefore she is to be delivered (cf. Hebrews 11:31). So here is God's grace being poured out in the midst of great judgement.

In addition, any precious metals, or implements made of precious metal, shall be taken and placed in the 'treasury of the LORD' (6:19). The term 'treasury' is often used in the Old Testament to refer to any gold, silver and utensils for the upkeep of the tabernacle or temple—that is, the house of the Lord (1 Kings 7:51; 15:18). These items are 'holy' to the Lord; the term 'holy' in Hebrew simply means that these objects are separated from common use and are set apart wholly to the Lord and his work.

The fall of Jericho (6:20-25)

The author of Joshua succinctly records the capture and destruction of Jericho by the Israelites in verses 20-21. This military rout occurs exactly as the angel of the Lord had outlined it in 6:2-5. The Israelites believe the word given by the angel of the Lord and now they act in obedience to carry out his orders. The writer of the book of Hebrews underscores their belief and obedience by saying, 'By faith the walls of Jericho fell down after they had been encircled for seven days' (Hebrews 11:30).

Just after the walls of the city fall, Joshua sends two spies, the same two who had reconnoitred the land in Joshua 2, to enter Jericho and deliver Rahab and her family from the destruction to come. There is dramatic irony in this act: Rahab had saved these two men from death, and now they do the same for her. The spies obey and retrieve Rahab and her family, and then they set them 'outside the camp of Israel'. This latter phrase is idiomatic in the Old Testament for the place of the ritually unclean. For example, the person suffering from leprosy 'shall remain unclean as long as he has the disease... His dwelling shall be outside the camp' (Leviticus 13:46). The priest takes the unclean parts of a sacrificial animal outside the camp of Israel to dispose of them because they are impure and defiled (Leviticus 4:11–12). Rahab and her family are ritually unclean Canaanites and, therefore, are barred from entrance into the community and into the tabernacle precincts. This state of uncleanness, however, is only temporary (see 6:25).

The section concludes with the statement that Rahab has lived in Israel since the time of the destruction of Jericho 'to this day' (6:25). This declaration serves as confirmation of the veracity of the account. In other words, the fall of Jericho took place exactly as the author has described it; if anyone has a question about its reliability, all they have to do is to ask Rahab, who is still living in Israel!

The curse on Jericho (6:26–27)
One final act completes the destruction of Jericho: Joshua pronounces that anyone who might endeavour to rebuild the city will be cursed. This curse is by no means a magical

incantation. Rather, Joshua speaks the word of the Lord, and it is the Lord alone who causes such things to come to pass (see Numbers 23:8). The curse is later fulfilled; we read in 1 Kings 16:34, 'In his days Hiel of Bethel built Jericho. He laid its foundation at the cost of Abiram his firstborn, and set up its gates at the cost of his youngest son Segub, according to the word of the LORD, which he spoke by Joshua the son of Nun.'

In contrast to the Lord's curse on Jericho in verse 26, we see the Lord's blessing on Joshua in verse 27. First, the text says that 'the LORD was with Joshua'; this phrase is an Old Testament formula to describe a person who is walking with the Lord and receiving his favour (see Genesis 39:2,23). Secondly, the text literally says that 'the report of his was in all the land'; this phrase underscores that Joshua and his actions at Jericho spread his fame and name throughout Canaan and elsewhere. Whereas Jericho is brought low and razed to the ground, Joshua is exalted and raised up in the land!

Points to ponder

1. God works in unexpected ways

We should be in awe of the manner of God's work in the fall of Jericho. God does things in his own way and in his own timing. His work is surprising. It is not done according to mankind's ways, but often in the most unexpected ways: 'For my thoughts are not your thoughts, neither are your ways my ways, declares the LORD' (Isaiah 55:8).

An interesting example is the call of William Carey to the mission field.[5] Two facts of Carey's life prior to his call are of interest: he was allergic to sunshine and he was a shoemaker (a worker in leather). These two characteristics should have barred his way to the mission field in India. But, as Appleby asks, 'Is it not surprising that someone allergic to sunshine and being a leather worker as well should have been sent by Providence to spend a lifetime in India where the former is constant and the latter is a trade of the despised lower caste?' God does not do things in the manner of men; we would consider Carey, in our day of assessing 'gifts', as perhaps one who would be unfit for missionary service. God knows better and, indeed, by using Carey the way he did, only brings more glory and honour to his own name. God's ways are not man's ways!

2. Mercy in the midst of judgement

The deliverance of Rahab and her family from the midst of the utter destruction of Jericho greatly exemplified God's grace coming in the midst of severe judgement. Indeed, God often saves his people in the very heart of evil and evil-doing.

For instance, in the eighteenth century, George Whitefield preached in the town of Rotherham in Yorkshire, and he was met with great hatred and loathing on the part of the crowd. He almost decided never to preach there again; however, he found out that some who had been bitter and terrible persecutors had been converted through his preaching and ministry in the town. One particular incident is telling.

Whitefield was held in such contempt in Rotherham that public bars became theatres in which the Bible, true religion and Whitefield were roundly ridiculed. At one of these public houses, a Mr Thrope and three of his companions decided to mimic Whitefield. A wager was made that the one who mimicked him the best would win the money. Thrope's three friends got up one by one on a table in the inn and did their best to ape Whitefield and to destroy everything sacred. Mr Thrope was the last to ascend the public-house pulpit. He exclaimed as he rose, 'I shall beat you all!' A Bible was handed to him, and, by the mysterious providence of God, it opened to Luke 13:3: 'Except ye repent, ye shall all likewise perish' (KJV).

As Thrope read the verse, great conviction came to his soul and he began to preach. And he preached with great earnestness. As he would later say, 'If ever I preached in my life by the assistance of the Spirit of God, it was at that time.' The crowd was struck dumb, not by entertainment but by Thrope's sincerity. Thrope was converted that hour by an unexampled act of divine grace and work. Later he became pastor of a church in Masborough, where he served for thirteen years until his death in 1776. Indeed, God can save and preserve his people even in the very mouth of the lion!

Defeat at Ai

Please read Joshua 7:1–26

The Puritan Jeremiah Burroughs wrote an important book called *A Treatise on Earthly-Mindedness.*[1] In this work Burroughs properly defines what 'earthly-mindedness' is. It is a scriptural term and concept: Philippians 3:19 says of the enemies of Christ that 'Their end is destruction, their god is their belly, and they glory in their shame, with minds set on earthly things.' These people are what the apostle John describes as 'those who dwell on the earth' (Revelation 3:10; 6:10; 8:13; 11:10).

'Earthly-mindedness' means that a person sets his mind and heart primarily on the things and cares of the world. He views the things of the world as the most excellent things, as if they are the real treasures of life and so should be pursued with ever so much vigour and fervour.

In Joshua 7 we are introduced to an 'earth-dweller'—that is, to one who loved the things of the world above even the promises of God. One in Israel had a heart enamoured with the pleasures, glory, beauty and pageantry of the earth!

A snake in the garden (7:1)

The narrative of the fall of Jericho in Joshua 6 describes a conquest that took place according to the word of the Lord. It went exactly according to plan. The Israelites obeyed, and conquered the city without a hitch. Even Rahab and her family were spared from the destruction, as the spies had promised earlier. Thus everything had gone smoothly. Or had it?

Things are not always what they seem to be on the surface. For here in verse 1 of chapter 7 a dark and ominous tone is set and delivered. The text says that Israel 'broke faith' with regard to the *cherem*; the verb 'to break faith' in Hebrew means that Israel acted 'treacherously' in the matter of the conquest of Jericho, much like a woman's infidelity to her husband (see Numbers 5:12,27). In other words, Israel did not keep God's word and command to them. The reason is stated clearly: Achan, a man from the tribe of Judah, took some of the items from Jericho that were either to be destroyed or to be deposited in the Lord's treasury, and he kept them for himself.

In this story we are introduced to the concept of covenant or corporate responsibility. In other words, the entire covenant community is responsible for the actions of its individual members. While Achan is the actual perpetrator of the sin, Israel as a whole must pay the price: '... the anger of the Lord burned against the people of Israel.'

Battle at Ai (7:2–5)

Israel discovers the sin of Achan by means of a military attack on the city of Ai. An analysis of the text reveals that the assault on Ai is parallel in structure to the attack on Jericho. As was the case at Jericho, Joshua sends spies to explore the region around the city of Ai. The Hebrew verb translated 'to spy out', used twice in verse 2, was used of the earlier reconnaissance of Jericho (6:25; and in noun form in 2:1; 6:23).

The location of the city of Ai is in dispute. It has traditionally been identified with the modern site of et-Tell, which is located in the central hill country about thirteen miles west of Jericho and approximately 3,500 feet (over 1,000 metres) higher in elevation. The site has been extensively excavated. The archaeological analysis of the site at et-Tell presents difficulties, however, because it does not match important events of biblical history, such as Joshua's campaign against it. It is therefore more likely that Ai is to be located at the nearby site of Khirbet el-Maqatir, which has undergone recent excavations.

In verse 3 the spies 'returned' to Joshua and provided a report. This also happened in the story of Jericho: the two spies 'returned' and told Joshua that the Lord had given the area of Jericho into their hands (2:23–24). Ai looks like an easy target, especially after the fall of the apparently formidable Jericho (see commentary on 6:1). The men of Ai 'are few' (7:3). In fact, the outcome of a battle at Ai is so obviously expected to be positive that the spies encourage Joshua to send only between two and three thousand men to attack the city.

It is at this point that the parallels between the attacks on Jericho and Ai end. The assault on Ai fails utterly as the Israelites 'fled before the men of Ai' (7:4). The warriors of Ai kill about thirty-six Israelites, and then they chase the rest from the gate of Ai to 'Shebarim'. Some translations treat 'Shebarim' as a proper name although its whereabouts is uncertain. In Hebrew the word is related to the verb 'to break' and, therefore, perhaps refers to the Israelite forces 'breaking apart' and running for their lives.

In the account of the fall of Jericho the author employs a metaphor that reflects the weak response of the Canaanites to the assault of Israel: their hearts melted before the Lord and Israel (2:11; 5:1; cf. 2:24). In an ironic turn of events, when Israel suffers defeat at Ai, 'the hearts of the [Israelite] people melted' (7:5).

In response to the defeat at Ai, Joshua and the elders of Israel enter into a time of mourning. They tear their garments and put dust on their heads, two common signs of bereavement (see Job 1:20; 2:12). In addition, they all bow before the ark of the covenant, and Joshua prays in an attempt to understand what has just happened to the army of Israel at Ai. This, of course, is the proper response. The reader should note, however, that at the outset of the Ai campaign neither Joshua nor the elders sought the Lord's direction or approval. Perhaps they had become complacent after the victory at Jericho, but their attention is secured with their defeat at Ai and they go before God in prayer and in humility.

Joshua's prayer, however, is misdirected. He seems to blame God for the reversal met by the Israelite troops at Ai. He asks whether the Lord has brought them into the land of Canaan in order to destroy them at the hands of the Amorites (7:7). This question is reminiscent of the Hebrews' response to the hard times they encountered in the wilderness wanderings (see Numbers 14:1–4). So Joshua queries God's motives without questioning the part that Israel may have played in the affair at Ai.

Christians in distress often ask the same question: 'O Lord, how could you allow this to happen to me?' While it is true that all things unfold according to God's providence, Christians yet need to gauge their own hearts and actions in each situation. Joshua does not ask the Lord, 'What did we do to deserve this reversal?' God, however, answers this question and explains it to him in no uncertain terms.

The problem (7:10–15)

The Lord commands Joshua to get up from his prayer and asks a question of his own: 'Why have you fallen on your face?' Then he firmly declares the reason for Israel's defeat at Ai: 'Israel has sinned' (7:11). God states this truth clearly. However, in verse 11 he expounds further, with great detail, the exact nature of Israel's sin. The Lord lists five parts to the sin; in the original Hebrew the phrase for each aspect of the sin begins with the words 'and also'. So, what did Israel do wrong? 'And also' they broke the covenant; 'and also' they took from the *cherem*, or devoted things; 'and also' they stole (i.e., silver and gold that belonged to God's treasury; see 7:21); 'and also' they lied; 'and also' they hid the things in their own tents. Israel has sinned greatly, and therefore 'Israel cannot stand before their enemies' (7:12).

Because Israel disobeyed God with regard to the *cherem*, Israel itself has become *cherem*. In an ironic fashion, the people of God have become just like that which they had been called to destroy, and so are subject to the same destruction. Such ironic reversal is common in the Scriptures. For example, in 2 Kings 17 the writer comments on the idolatrous practices of the Israelites—things which God had repeatedly told them not to do—by saying, 'They went after false idols and became false' (v. 15; cf. Psalm 115:4–8).

God then threatens the Israelites that he will no longer be with them unless they root out the problem (7:12–13). He goes on to enumerate the various steps that Israel must take to resolve the issue. First, they must prepare for the next day by 'consecrating' themselves (7:13). In other words, they must purify themselves, which is probably done by washing their clothes and abstaining from sexual relations (see commentary on 3:1–6). Secondly, all Israel are to gather in the morning before the Lord according to their tribal families. The Lord will at that time designate the tribe to which the culprit belongs, then the clan and, finally, the household. The household that is identified by the Lord will step forward on its own.

The method that God uses to indicate his choices is not stated in the text. Verse 14 simply reads that 'the LORD takes', or 'seizes'. Some commentators believe the Lord's intentions are delivered to the people by lots. The ESV, for example, reads, 'the LORD takes by lot,' adding 'by lot' to its translation although it is not in the Hebrew text. Perhaps God uses Urim and Thummim from the high priest's breastpiece to reveal God's decisions on particular important matters (Exodus 28:30; Numbers 27:21). Or maybe the Lord simply speaks to convey his wishes to the people.

The one who is named, and all that belongs to him, shall be burned with fire. This is exactly what happened to Jericho: 'And they burned the city with fire, and everything in it' (6:24). Ironically, the culprit will receive the same treatment as the pagan people of Jericho. In a sense, he has become one of them and, therefore, he has come under the *cherem*.

The confession (7:16–21)

Joshua obeys the word of the Lord and he gathers the tribes of Israel the next morning. The Lord identifies the culprit: he is Achan of the Zerahite clan of the tribe of Judah. This tribal disclosure is quite striking since Judah is the leading tribe of Israel at the time. In Genesis 49:8–12, Jacob blessed Judah by saying that he will rule over his brothers, and the great king of Israel will come from his line. The tribe of Judah receives the first allotment of land in Canaan (15:1). After the death of Joshua it is the tribe of Judah that leads the final conquest of Canaan (Judges 1:1–2). Yet Judah will now bear the ignominy of having broken the *cherem*.

In verses 14–18 of this chapter the verb 'to take' appears eight times. This repetition is what German biblical scholars call the use of a *Leitwort*, namely, a 'leading word', or keyword. A *Leitwort* often provides keen insight into the sense of a passage. This verb is not the common one in Hebrew for 'to take', but rather it is primarily a military term that means 'to capture', or 'seize'. The author of Joshua uses the same verb to describe the Israelite 'capture' of Jericho (6:20) and Ai (8:19,21). The *Leitwort* emphasizes that the culprit, or breaker of the *cherem*, is captured and destroyed just like the pagan cities of Jericho and Ai.

Joshua confronts Achan and encourages him to confess what he did with regard to the *cherem*. In fact, the verb translated 'give praise' in verse 19 can bear the idea of confession in the Hebrew language (see Ezra 10:11). Achan answers Joshua truthfully: he says that he had seen among the spoils of Jericho a beautiful cloak from Shinar (i.e., Mesopotamia), 200 shekels of silver and an ingot of gold worth fifty shekels, and, being lured by these objects, Achan simply 'took them' (7:21). Achan, in addition, clearly understands the reason he acted this way—he says, 'I coveted them' (7:21) and 'I have sinned against the LORD' (7:20).

Achan accurately defines his own sin: he coveted. Coveting may properly be understood as an inordinate, ungoverned, selfish desire for something that belongs to someone else. The Hebrew word used here for 'covet' is the same verb used in Genesis 3:6 of Eve's unquenchable desire and thirst for the fruit of the forbidden tree. She had an unbridled passion for, and obsession with, the Lord's property. Covetousness occurs when the world enters the heart; as Thomas Watson comments, it is an 'insatiable desire of getting the world ... an inordinate love of the world'. Saint Augustine called it 'to desire more than enough'. The world becomes the coveter's idol, and so it was with Achan.

We are all well aware of how alluring and tempting riches can be. We need to guard our hearts, for 'where your treasure is, there your heart will be also' (Matthew 6:21). The story is told of John Newton, the famous hymn-writer, that one day he was called to visit a family in his congregation who had suffered the loss of all that they had by a devastating fire. Newton found the pious mistress of the house and he saluted her with the statement: 'I give you joy, madam!' Surprised and offended, the woman replied, 'What! Joy that all my property has been consumed?' 'Oh, no,' Newton answered, 'but joy that you have so much property that fire cannot touch.' This allusion to her real treasure checked the woman's grief, and she wiped away her tears. She, as a Christian, knew that what the minister said was true.

It is important for us to recognize that recognition of one's guilt and confession of one's sin do not erase or expunge the consequences or penalties due to the sinful activity. Man cannot say, 'I am sorry,' and have life return to normal without any effects from the sin. It's not, as we used to say as children in the game of hide-and-seek, 'all-ye, all-ye, in-free'! There are temporal consequences to sin. It is good that Achan confessed, but that does not absolve him of responsibility for his actions.

The penalty (7:22–26)
The defeat at Ai provokes a sense of urgency to address the sin that brought about the rout. So Joshua sends some attendants to Achan's tent to see whether the goods are hidden there. The men run to the tent and they find the goods exactly where Achan said they would be (7:22).

Once the evidence is produced, Joshua and all Israel gather together Achan and everything that belongs to him, which includes his family, possessions and the stolen goods. They take them all and place them in the Valley of Achor. The assembly point is located outside the camp of Israel, which is the place of the unclean (see commentary on 6:20–25). The valley-name Achor literally means 'trouble' in Hebrew, and serves as a wordplay on the name of the culprit Achan. The author of 1 Chronicles is well aware of this play on a name when he says, 'The son of Carmi: Achan, the troubler of Israel, who broke faith in the matter of the devoted thing' (1 Chr. 2:7).[2] The word the author uses for 'troubler' is Achor. Joshua uses the same wordplay in verse 25 of our text.

Modern readers often have trouble understanding why everything belonging to Achan is taken outside the camp of Israel and destroyed. It does not seem fair. Joshua 6:21 provides a clue to the issue, saying that everything belonging to the city of

Jericho is laid waste; many of the same items listed as destroyed at Jericho are destroyed in the Valley of Achor. What we see is that Achan broke the *cherem*, and now he is the object of the *cherem*. He really is no different from a pagan from the city of Jericho!

All of Israel then killed the humans and animals by stoning, and burned everything with fire. As stated previously, the city of Jericho and everything in it had also been burned with fire (6:24). This parallel further supports the claim that Achan, like the city of Jericho, is an object of the *cherem*.

Finally, Israel builds a heap of stones on top of the remains in the valley. In the following chapter of Joshua, the people do the same thing to the Canaanite king of Ai (8:29). In both instances the text says that the heaps are still standing 'to this day'—that is, at the time of the writing of the book. The heaps are thus symbols to remind Israel of what happened at these sites and to warn them not to act in a similar way.

Points to ponder

1. Where is our treasure?
The story of Achan poses the question to each one of us: 'Where is my heart? Upon what do I principally place my mind and heart?' Jesus tells us, 'For where your treasure is, there your heart will be also' (Matthew 6:21). One way to gauge our hearts in this matter is to ask ourselves, 'What is upon my heart in times of solitude?' When I am alone and need not impress anyone else, what is it that I place my heart on? It is at these times that the true nature of my wants and desires can be discovered.

We understand that all people have earthly needs: air, food, clothing, relationships and shelter. No one denies this fact. But the difference between the earthly-minded man and the man who is spiritually-minded is that the former makes earthly things the centre of reality. The godly person does not make such things the end-all; the godly man strives for something higher and better—that is, the more excellent things. The author of Hebrews tells us, 'For here we have no lasting city, but we seek the city that is to come' (Hebrews 13:14). There is something that is richer and more glorious than the things of the earth.

Another way to measure the state of our hearts is to ask the question: 'How do I spend my time? Is my time primarily concerned with earthly cares? What do I do with my time?' I fear many of us miss the spires of the heavenly city because we are so busy building earthly mansions. The king of France was once asked about an eclipse that had recently occurred. He answered, 'I have so much business in the earth that I take little notice of the things of heaven.'

2. What can we do to avoid being earthly-minded?
We all cling to the earth to one degree or another. Let me give you a few suggestions to help loosen our grip.

First, we ought to *employ the means of grace that God has given to the church for this very purpose.* He has given us the Scriptures to fortify us; he has given us prayer to strengthen us; he has given us worship to make us healthy Christians; he has given us fellowship with other believers to increase our sanctification. We need to take advantage of these wonderful blessings, and we need to guard our souls with them. They help to put us on the right path.

Secondly, we ought to *set the example of Jesus before our eyes* and in our hearts and thoughts. We should take to heart how he lived and what was important to him. Sanctification and being heavenly-minded are characteristics of believers in the process of becoming more and more like Jesus.

Finally, *let us remind ourselves repeatedly about our true condition in the world as believers.* The earth is not our home, but we are pilgrims and strangers here. Paul reminds us of this truth when he says, 'our citizenship is in heaven' (Philippians 3:20). The writer to the Hebrews describes the people of faith in the Old Testament in the following way:

These all died in faith, not having received the things promised, but having seen them and greeted them from afar, and having acknowledged that they were strangers and exiles on the earth. For people who speak thus make it clear that they are seeking a homeland. If they had been thinking of that land from which they had gone out, they would have had opportunity to return. But as it is, they desire a better country, that is, a heavenly one. Therefore God is not ashamed to be called their God, for he has prepared for them a city (Hebrews 11:13–16).

10

Defeat of Ai

Please read Joshua 8:1–29

When the Israelites first attacked the city of Ai it was a failure (7:2–5). Of course, the major reason that Israel failed was that Achan had stolen some of the goods from Jericho that had come under the ban (*cherem*). Another problem emerges from the text which appears to have also contributed to the Israelite defeat in battle. It should be noted that in 7:2–3 Joshua made the decision and gave orders for the assault on Ai. The text never states that Joshua and the Israelites consulted God in the matter. The campaign failed partly because it lacked divine sanction and direction. The Israelites became proud and complacent after the recent victory at Jericho, and so they engaged the army of Ai in battle under their own strength and power. Hubris was another reason for their failure. Calvin put it this way: 'The most effective poison to lead men to ruin is to boast in themselves, in their own wisdom and willpower.'

Once after Charles Spurgeon had given a particularly powerful sermon, he was standing at the door of the church greeting people. A man came up to him, gushing and saying, 'That was the greatest sermon I ever heard! And you are the greatest preacher alive!' Spurgeon looked at the man and said, 'Yes, the devil told me that ten minutes ago!' Whether or not this story is true (some stories about Spurgeon are questionable), the point is well made. As Christians, we need to be careful of pride and an attitude of self-sufficiency. Spurgeon elsewhere told his students that they needed to help the people in their congregations to look up to Jesus —with both eyes!

God's command for battle (8:1–2)
In the present passage the Israelites are to attack the city of Ai a second time. In contrast to the first battle, the Lord commands Israel to fight, and he even tells them how to proceed.

First, the Lord encourages Joshua by saying, 'Do not fear and do not be dismayed.' This is a common opening clause when God orders the Israelites to military action in Canaan (see Deuteronomy 1:21; 31:8; Joshua 10:25; cf. 1:9). Obviously the Israelites would have been hesitant and fearful because of their recent setback in the first battle of Ai (7:5).

Secondly, God tells Joshua to take 'all the fighting men' to the battle; in the first attack only 3,000 warriors participated in the engagement (7:4).

Finally, in the first battle the Israelites were confident of victory because of their recent triumph over Jericho and the apparent weakness of the defenders of Ai. They were, however, soundly thrashed. Now Israel holds a well-founded confidence.

The conquest of Ai is to involve only a partial *cherem*. Later in the chapter Joshua 'devoted all the inhabitants of Ai to destruction' (8:26). However, according to God's command in verse 2, the Israelites are allowed to plunder Ai and to keep the spoil which they capture. Jericho, in contrast, was placed under a fully-fledged *cherem* in which everything was either to be destroyed or put in the Lord's treasury.

The final order of the Lord to Joshua concerns the method of attack. The Israelites are to 'lay an ambush against the city' (8:2). This military manoeuvre differs from the first battle, when the Israelite forces made an all-out assault on the front gate of the city (7:5). The Lord controls this second battle, and he directs the attack and the outcome.

Setting the ambush (8:3–9)
Joshua obeys the Lord by setting up the ambush. He chooses 30,000 elite forces for the ambush: the epithet 'mighty men of valour' is commonly used in the Old Testament of people who are valiant and are particularly skilled in the craft of warfare (see Judges 6:12; 1 Samuel 16:18; 2 Kings 5:1). Joshua sends these troops to the hiding-place 'by night': secrecy and stealth are important factors in the success of an ambush. He then tells the warriors where they are to lie in wait. The spot is 'behind' the city; verse 9 provides more information to this placement by saying it is west of Ai and east of Bethel. The forces are to remain close to Ai, and they are to be prepared and ready for battle (8:4).

The plan then calls for Joshua and some of the remaining troops to approach the city of Ai from the front—that is, towards the location of the main city-gate. This movement is to echo the first Israelite assault on Ai recorded in 7:2–5. Joshua and his men will flee before the soldiers of Ai in the same manner as in the first attack (7:5). But, in reality, their flight is merely a feint, or decoy, to draw Ai's forces away from the city. With the enemy forces drawn away from the gate, the Israelite troops in ambush will be free to enter the city, capture it and burn it.

Joshua speaks with true confidence because 'the LORD your God will give it' into the hands of the Hebrew army. His assurance is evident in his speech: he begins with the imperative 'See!' (the ESV translates it as 'Behold!', 8:4). And Joshua ends his oration with the same volitional 'See!' (8:8). These two imperatives form an *inclusio*; in other words, they bracket both ends of the speech. Joshua is clear and certain that this ambush will succeed because it is from the Lord, and the Israelites will see it happen.

The feint (8:10–17)

Joshua now begins to put the plan into action. He takes all the army and they encamp in front of the city of Ai with a ravine separating them from the city. He then sends 5,000 soldiers to lie in ambush at the rear, or west, of the city. Thus a large force remains encamped with Joshua to the north of Ai, and a smaller force lies in wait behind the city.

How do we harmonize this force of 5,000 men with the command in verses 3–4 that places the number of soldiers for the ambush at 30,000? It is likely that the figure of 30,000 men reflects the total size of Joshua's army that he is actively using against Ai (that is ten times the number of the first assault on the city, see 7:4). In other words, 5,000 soldiers are set in ambush and the remaining 25,000 are with Joshua to feign a frontal assault on Ai.

When the king of Ai sees the Israelite force in front of the city, he senses victory in his grasp, just like at the first battle of Ai (7:5). So he musters the army and goes out to meet the Israelites in battle 'towards the Arabah'. In this context, the Arabah is the area of the Jordan Valley just west of the Jordan River (see Deuteronomy 11:30; 2 Samuel 2:29). From Ai, the Arabah is to the east, so the troops under Joshua flee to the east as they are being pursued by the army of Ai. In this manner, the forces of Ai are being 'drawn away from the city' (8:16) to the east while the Israelite ambush force is lying in wait to the west of the city. The city is ripe for picking.

The leadership of the city of Bethel, which is next to Ai, sees an opportunity to join in the rout of the Israelite army. So they send all their soldiers in pursuit of Joshua's forces to the east (8:17).

The capture of Ai (8:18–23)
In contrast to the first attack on the city of Ai, the Lord directs the battle plan. He gives direct orders to Joshua to 'Stretch out the javelin that is in your hand towards Ai' (8:18). This command is reminiscent of ones that the Lord gave to Aaron and Moses during the events relating to the plagues in Egypt and the wanderings in the wilderness (Exodus 7:19; 8:5; 10:21; 14:16). In the present case the raising of the javelin serves as a signal for the ambush to begin.

In response, the 5,000 men lying in wait move quickly to run into the city (8:19). They capture the city immediately and then they hurry to set it on fire. Speed is of the essence because the army of Ai has been drawn away from the city but could return at a moment's notice. The soldiers of Ai, however, do not realize that the withdrawal of the Israelite army was a feint until they see the smoke rising up from the city; by then it is too late.

The Israelite forces under Joshua's command also see the city burning. At this sight, the 25,000 troops turn to face the army of Ai and then they attack them (8:21). At the same time the 5,000 Israelite soldiers inside Ai rush out and strike the enemy from behind. The army of Ai is caught in the jaws of a military vice with nowhere to flee. The Israelite army then crushes and demolishes it (8:22). The entirety of the enemy is destroyed; not one soldier remains alive. Yet there is one exception: the Israelites capture the king of Ai and they bring him into the presence of Joshua.

The conclusion (8:24–29)

After the Israelite army utterly destroys the forces of the Canaanites of Ai—having killed every soldier in the field—they now enter the city and slay all the inhabitants remaining there. Apparently when the force of 5,000 had captured the city and burned it, they had not killed all the inhabitants (8:19). The sum of those who are slain that day, in the field and in the city, is 12,000 people; this number is 'all the people of Ai' (8:25).

At the outset of the engagement, Joshua stretched out his javelin towards Ai; previously we concluded that this gesture served to signal the beginning of the ambush (8:18–19). However, in verse 26, we are told that the act means more than merely the start of the conflict: Joshua holds up the javelin in his hand until all the people of the city of Ai had fallen (8:26). This action is reminiscent of an earlier battle between Israel and the Amalekites at Rephidim (Exodus 17:8–16). During that battle, when Moses held up 'his hand' Israel dominated the battle, but when he rested 'his hand' the Amalekites held sway

(Exodus 17:11). Moses held God's rod in his hand. 'The rod is the mediating instrument of God's power. It is God who is fighting for Israel, and he who is to be glorified. And the reason Israel does not prevail when the rod is lowered is to show the people that God contributes more to their victory than do sword and shield.' It is likely that Joshua's raising up a javelin and holding it up throughout the entire battle of Ai has the same purpose: to demonstrate that Israel is victorious through the power of God.

As stated above, the defeat of Ai involves only a partial *cherem*. The Israelite invaders keep for themselves the livestock and goods of the city; only the human inhabitants are utterly destroyed (8:27). Joshua then orders the city to be totally burned down so that it would be 'a heap of ruins' for ever. The author comments that this heap remains 'to this day', namely, to the day of the composition of the book.

One matter remains for the conquering Israelites to settle: what to do with the king of Ai whom they had captured. He is summarily executed, and his doom serves as an example and symbol. First, the Israelites hang the king to death on a tree. Then they remove his corpse at the end of the day, and they hurl it at the very entrance of the main gate of the city of Ai. Finally, the people place 'a great heap of stones' on top of the king's body. This last act is the same as what the Israelites did to Achan's body (7:26). Both heaps of stones are monuments, but they are memorials to contrasting attitudes and actions. The heap piled up over the body of Achan represents Israel's sin and their breaking of faith with regard to the *cherem*. The heap over the king of Ai symbolizes Israel's obedience to God and testifies to their restoration.

Points to ponder

The importance of obeying God's word

In the second battle of Ai, Joshua and the Israelites obey the Lord's command precisely. Thus they are triumphant through the power of God. The church needs people who obey the word of God exactly and obey God's calling to them.

Adoniram Judson, after graduating from seminary, received a call from a very influential church in Boston; he was invited to come and be its assistant pastor. Many people congratulated him on receiving such a desirable offer and position. However, Judson responded unexpectedly by saying, 'My call is not here. God is calling me beyond the seas. To stay here, even to serve God in His ministry, I feel would be only partial obedience, and I could not be happy in that.' The *Forward* magazine reported after Judson's death that 'The fashionable church in Boston still stands, rich and strong, but Judson's [reformed Baptist] churches in Burma [now called Myanmar] have fifty thousand converts, and the influence of his life is felt around the world.' Patrick Johnstone in *Operation World* estimates that in Myanmar's Baptist Convention today there are 3,700 congregations with 617,781 members and 1,900,000 affiliates.[2] Adoniram Judson was the first missionary to enter Myanmar's unreached area with the gospel. God does not want people of 'partial obedience', but rather he wants those who obey him and keep his word.

11

Covenant renewal

Please read Joshua 8:30–35

Immediately before Israel invaded the land of promise the people were encamped in the plains of Moab in Transjordan. There Moses expounded upon the law that God had first revealed at Mount Sinai. Moses' exposition of the Torah is recorded in the book of Deuteronomy. Towards the end of his exposition, in Deuteronomy 27:1–8, Moses commanded the elders of Israel that when the people of God crossed into the land of Canaan they were to conduct a covenant renewal ceremony. As a central part of that ritual, Israel would place a new copy of the terms of the covenant (i.e., the law) upon Mount Ebal. The people were then to recite to one another the blessings and curses of the covenant while standing on Mount Gerizim and Mount Ebal. The passage we have now reached in the book of Joshua is the fulfilment of Moses' earlier directives for Israel to perform this covenant-renewal ceremony.

This ceremony primarily underscores the truth that the Word of God is at the very heart of Israel's existence. It is to be Israel's first priority. And all Israel, every person, whether native or sojourner, is to participate in the renewal ritual. 'All the people of God must give all obedience to all the word of God.'[1] The Word of God is the very lifeblood of the people of God. As Guthrie comments:

> It is an armoury of heavenly weapons, a laboratory of infallible medicines, a mine of exhaustless wealth. It is a guidebook for every road, a chart for every sea, a medicine for every malady, a balm for every wound. Rob us of our Bible, and our sky has lost its sun, and in the best of other books we have naught but the glimmer of twinkling stars. It is the wealth of the poor, blessing poverty with the contentment which makes it rich. It is the shield of wealth, protecting the few that are rich against the many that are poor. It may be compared to the skies, which hold at once the most blessed and the most baneful elements—soft dews to bathe the opening rose and bolts that rend the oak asunder.[2]

Building an altar (8:30–31)

The first act of Joshua in the covenant-renewal ceremony is to construct an altar to the Lord, something that Moses had commanded Israel to do (Deuteronomy 27:5–7). They are to place it on Mount Ebal.

> This is a special altar for the extraordinary occasion of covenant ratification. The stones for the altar ... are not to be worked but they are to be uncut fieldstones. This is in agreement with the statute of Exodus 20:25, which says, 'If you make an altar of stones for me, you shall not build it

[of] hewn stones, because you will wield your tool upon it, and you will defile it.' The reasons for this prohibition are twofold: first, it is a polemic against Canaanite altars, which were made primarily out of cut, finished stone. Secondly, the Hebrews are not to wield a tool in erecting an altar so that they will not be tempted into making an idol.[3]

Moses also commanded Israel that on this special occasion they are to offer burnt offerings and peace offerings on the altar on Mount Ebal (Deuteronomy 27:6–7).

Mount Ebal and its counterpart Mount Gerizim are located in the central hill-country. They sit approximately twenty miles north of the city of Ai along the 'spine', or central ridge, of the highlands. The city of Shechem lies between the two mountains, and stood as an important city in the life of the patriarchs of Israel (Genesis 12:6; 33:18–20; 34:1–31). The text does not indicate that Israel under Joshua had to fight for the territory of Shechem in which the covenant renewal takes place; perhaps the Canaanite inhabitants passively submitted to the Israelites.

Standing stones (8:32)
The 'stones' mentioned in this verse are not the 'stones' of the altar spoken of in verses 30–31. Rather, these are standing stones that Moses had commanded Israel to establish when the people entered the land of Canaan. He said:

And on the day you cross over the Jordan to the land that the LORD your God is giving you, you shall set up large stones and plaster them with plaster. And you shall write on them all the words of this law... And ... you shall set up these stones ... on Mount Ebal (Deuteronomy 27:2–4).

The raising up of these large standing stones is part of the ceremony of covenant renewal. The people are to coat the stones with white plaster and to inscribe upon them the law. 'The white plaster provides a backdrop against which the writing may be seen clearly and distinctly (see [Deuteronomy] 27:8).'[4] What is written on the stones is the 'law of Moses'. It is not clear how much of the law this includes: some believe it is only the Decalogue; others think it is select portions of Deuteronomy; and yet others hold that it refers to the entire book of Deuteronomy.

Israel on the mountains (8:33)

The third step of the ceremony is the positioning of the tribes of Israel on the two mountains. Moses gave directions for half the tribes to stand on Mount Gerizim as a symbol of blessing, and the other half of the tribes to stand on Mount Ebal as a sign of cursing (Deuteronomy 27:11-13). This ceremonial act in the book of Joshua is a fulfilment of Deuteronomy 11:29, which says, 'And when the LORD your God brings you into the land that you are entering to take possession of it, you shall set the blessing on Mount Gerizim and the curse on Mount Ebal.' The Levites then carry the ark of the covenant as detailed in the law (Numbers 4:15), and set it in the valley between the two groups on the two mountains. Its central position in the ceremony demonstrates its centrality to the very life of the people.

The final act of covenant renewal (8:34-35)

In the last step of the ritual, Joshua reads 'all the words of the law, the blessing and the curse', to the people even as they stand separated on the two mountains to represent the blessing and curse of the law. The passage which Joshua reads to the people is probably Deuteronomy 27:15-28:68, which is a long series of maledictions and blessings to come upon Israel depending on whether or not they are obedient to the covenant. Sanctions like these are a common element of ancient Near-Eastern covenants. When a partner in a treaty is obedient to the laws of the covenant, blessings will abound upon him; if he is disobedient, then curses will rain down on him.

Points to ponder

The Scriptures ought to be at the very core of our Christian walk and the life of the church
We ought to love and obey the Bible. J. C. Ryle once commented:

Love to the Word has been a prominent feature in the history of all the saints, of whom we know anything, since the days of the Apostles. This is the lamp that Athanasius and Chrysostom and Augustine followed. This is the compass that kept the Waldensians and Albigenses from making shipwreck of the faith. This is the well that was reopened by Wycliffe and Luther, after it had been long stopped up. This is the sword with which Latimer, and Jewell, and Knox won their victories. This is the manna which fed Baxter and Owen, and the noble host of the Puritans, and made them strong in battle. This is the armoury from which Whitefield and Wesley drew their powerful weapons. This is the mine from which Bickersteth and M'Cheyne brought forth rich gold. Differing as these holy men did in some matters, on one point they were all agreed—they all delighted in the Word.[5]

We today ignore the Scriptures to our own detriment and doom. As Ryle comments elsewhere:

... much of religious error may be traced to ignorance of the Bible... The truth of the principle here laid down is proved by facts in almost every age of church history. The reformation in Josiah's day was closely connected with the discovery of the book of the law. The false doctrines of the Jews in our Lord's time were the result of neglecting the Scriptures. The dark ages of Christendom were times when the Bible was kept back from the people. The Protestant Reformation was mainly effected by translating and circulating the Bible. The churches which are most flourishing at this day are churches which honour the Bible. The nations which enjoy most moral light are nations in which the Bible is most known. The parishes in our land where there is most true religion are those in which the Bible is most studied. The godliest families are Bible-reading families. The holiest men and women are Bible-reading people. These are simple facts that cannot be denied.[6]

Spurgeon commented that 'Your neglected Bible hides your God.'

12

Covenant with the Gibeonites

Please read Joshua 9:1–27

udson Taylor, the great missionary to China during the nineteenth century, was once asked by his wife, 'Are you proud of anything?' He answered, 'Proud about what?' She said, 'The many things you have done and accomplished.' He responded, 'I never knew I had done anything.' Hudson Taylor clearly understood that any success in ministry or in the Christian walk is by the power, work and grace of Jesus Christ. Man's own efficacy or capacity cannot engender success. Only Christ is all-powerful and all-sufficient. Spurgeon's words echo through the ages: 'If Christ be anything, he must be everything!'

Unfortunately, many of us in the church grasp our own seeming self-sufficiency; there is a lingering pride in who we are and what we can accomplish. When we face a problem we often seek to solve it in our own strength. This response is, of course, nothing new for the people of God in history. In Joshua 7

Israel attempted to capture Ai without consulting the Lord and, thus, to do it in their own strength. After the army's victory over Jericho the people thought they would easily conquer the small site of Ai. It would be a piece of cake! In the event, the Israelite forces were humbled and humiliated by the soldiers of Ai. In the present episode in Joshua 9 we encounter the same old story: the Israelites engage in a covenant with the pagan Gibeonites without consulting the Lord or seeking his approval

The initial reaction of the Canaanites (9:1-2)

When the inhabitants of the land of Canaan 'heard' of the Israelite invasion of the central highlands, their kings mobilized forces to fight against the intruders. The kings of six people groups are listed: 'the Hittites, the Amorites, the Canaanites, the Perizzites, the Hivites, and the Jebusites'. In Joshua 3:10, seven nations were listed as inhabiting the land; the extra group in this earlier passage is the Girgashites. A listing of the peoples that dwell in the land of promise appears ten times in the Pentateuch, and a majority of the references mention less than seven groups. The point of the list in the present context is to indicate that there is a general, widespread military response by all the peoples of Canaan. And, indeed, they are acting 'as one', or in one accord.

A different reaction (9:3-5)

When the Gibeonites 'heard' (the same verb as in 9:1) that Israel had attacked the land, they respond in a peculiar, unique way. Rather than dealing with Israel by force, in marked contrast to their fellow Canaanites, the Gibeonites resort to 'cunning', or 'craftiness'. Verse 4 begins with, 'they on their part acted with cunning', signifying a comparison between the Gibeonites and Joshua: just as Joshua acts cleverly and calculatingly in the defeat of Ai, so now the Gibeonites act shrewdly with Joshua in order to survive.

The Gibeonites begin their deception by masquerading themselves and their animals. The use of the adjective 'worn-out' four times in verses 4–5 underscores the disguise they fabricate. The clothes they wear, the sandals on their feet and the sacks and skins which their donkeys carry are all tattered and threadbare. The food that they carry is to be dry and crumbly. The Gibeonites concoct the trickery so that when they meet with Joshua and Israel it will appear that they have travelled a long way—in other words, from a distant country (see 9:6). The reality, of course, is different: Gibeon is located in the central highlands of Canaan, a mere six miles north-west of Jerusalem and only five miles south-west of Ai.[1] Gibeon lies in the region in which the Israelites have been waging war.

The ruse (9:6–13)

The Gibeonites travel to the Israelite camp at Gilgal to meet with Joshua. The distance from Gibeon to Gilgal is approximately fifteen miles to the east. When the Gibeonites arrive at Gilgal they lie to the Israelites by claiming that they have come 'from a distant country' (9:6). They then demand that the Israelites make a 'covenant', or treaty, with them. The Gibeonites appear to be aware of the injunction that Moses had given to the people of Israel with regard to the conquest of Canaan:

> When the LORD your God brings you into the land that you are entering to take possession of it, and clears away many nations before you, the Hittites, the Girgashites, the Amorites, the Canaanites, the Perizzites, the Hivites, and the Jebusites, seven nations more numerous and mightier than

yourselves, and when the LORD your God gives them over
to you, and you defeat them, then you must devote them
to complete destruction. You shall make no covenant with
them and show no mercy to them (Deuteronomy 7:1–2).

A prominent aspect of the Gibeonite deception is their claim
that they are not from Canaan, but from a faraway land. The
reality is that the Gibeonites are 'Hivites' (9:7) and, therefore, are
part of a people group that God had designated for destruction
by Israel (cf. Deuteronomy 20:10–18).

The Israelites are initially suspicious. They too are well aware
of Moses' command that they are not to make a covenant with
any of the peoples of Canaan. Therefore, Joshua presses the
Gibeonites, directly asking who they are and where they come
from. The Gibeonites add to their deceit by answering that they
have come from a 'very' distant land; the use of the adjective
'very' in Hebrew is to reflect intensity in degree or magnitude.
They are claiming to be from an exceedingly great distance.
They allay the suspicions of the Israelites by announcing that
they are in servitude to Israel, a statement that proves to be a
self-fulfilling prophecy (see 9:23).

The Gibeonites then attempt to provide a theological
justification for their overtures to the Israelites. They have heard
a report of the Lord's actions in Egypt and in dealing with the
Amorite kings, and now they declare that they have travelled
to Gilgal 'because of the name of the LORD your God' (9:9).
Here they employ the name 'Yahweh', which is the personal,
covenantal name that the Lord had revealed to his own people.
The inhabitants of Jericho had heard the same reports as the
Gibeonites, but they had reacted differently. Their hearts had
melted, yet they resisted and did not engage with Israel in

negotiations or in a covenant (2:10–11). Some non-Israelites respond with joy and worship of the Lord when they hear the reports of his work in Egypt (Exodus 18:11; Joshua 2:11). Thus it would not be odd if the Gibeonites were to respond in the same way. It seems, however, that the Gibeonites' theological statement is merely part of the ruse to escape the sword of Israel!

Finally, the Gibeonites provide physical support and confirmation for their story that they have travelled from a long distance to make a covenant with Israel. They produce bread that is 'dry and crumbly' (9:12), wineskins that have 'burst' and clothes and sandals that have 'worn out' (9:13). Compounding their deceit, the Gibeonites explain to the Israelites that when they set out from their homes, the bread was still warm and the wineskins were full.

A covenant with the Gibeonites (9:14–15)

The meaning of the opening clause of verse 14, 'the men took some of their provisions', is uncertain. Perhaps it indicates that the Israelites examine the Gibeonite provisions to see whether they are telling the truth. On the basis of that evidence, the leaders of Israel then make a covenant with the Gibeonites. Other commentators argue that the taking of the provisions is 'tantamount to a covenant ritual involving a communal eating of bread, intended to seal an agreement. This is an intriguing suggestion; Genesis 31:46–47 also speaks of a meal that concludes a covenant ceremony.'[2] In reality, the former interpretation is preferable since the clause, 'the men took some of their provisions', is connected to the statement in verse 14 that these same men did not seek counsel from the Lord in the matter of the covenant. The Israelites are acting on the physical evidence before them rather than on the word of the Lord.

Self-reliance is the reason that Israel is duped. They act on their own and do not seek the Lord's will. So, acting on the basis of the Gibeonites' word, Joshua makes a covenant with them; the promises of this treaty are peace and life to the Gibeonites. Joshua, however, does not act alone in this matter—the leaders of Israel take part in swearing the oath of the covenant (9:15).

Confrontation (9:16–20)

After the formalization of the covenant agreement the Gibeonites return to their homes (9:17 implies this). But after three days the Israelites become aware of the ruse they have perpetrated—the text does not tell the reader how the Israelites found out, but certainly the World War II adage applies: 'Loose lips sink ships'! They 'heard' that the Gibeonites actually lived nearby within the land of Canaan. Israel immediately responds by travelling to the cities of the Gibeonites, reaching them 'on the third day', with the intention of confronting them with their deception.

We learn for the first time that the Gibeonites do not only inhabit the city of Gibeon, but that their settlement area includes four cities. Gibeon is the main city of the coalition, but the colony also includes Chephirah, Beeroth and Kiriath-jearim. These latter towns span from Gibeon in an arch to the west and south; thus when we speak of the Gibeonite settlement we ought to think in terms of a region rather than a mere single-city habitation.

The Israelite army does not attack the Gibeonites because the Israelite leaders had sworn an oath as part of the covenant. One of the stipulations of that oath is that the lives of the Gibeonites would be spared (9:15,20). God requires covenant oaths to be kept (see Genesis 26:26–31; 2 Samuel 21:7; Ezekiel 16:59–60), and Israel abides by the word that has been given. The general population of Israel does not like it, and so 'all the congregation' murmurs and grumbles against their leadership. This is the precise language used of the complaining Israelites during the wilderness wanderings (Exodus 15:24; 16:2; Numbers 14:36; 17:5). They are probably discontented in the present episode because they want revenge and the spoils of the Gibeonite towns!

To their credit, the Israelite leaders keep their word given in the covenant and spare the lives of the Gibeonites. However, this does not mean the Gibeonites evade the consequences of their deceit. As a result of their guile and lying, they become cutters of wood and drawers of water for the whole congregation of Israel. Those two occupations are mentioned together in Deuteronomy 29:11, to reflect the lowliest types of work. In that passage there 'is presented a careful list of all those who make up the community of Israel, beginning with the leadership and ending with the lowliest servants who chop wood and draw water. In other words, the list is in descending order from the highest office down to the most menial position.'³ The Gibeonites may have survived the Israelite conquest of Canaan, but they end up being relegated to the lowest rank in society. And, as far as we know, they are never truly integrated into Israelite culture. In 2 Samuel 21:2 the text reads, 'Now the Gibeonites were not of the people of Israel but of the remnant of the Amorites.' This latter statement is made some four centuries after the episode of Joshua 9.

The encounter (9:22–27)
Joshua summons the Gibeonites to come before him and to give an account of their deceptive dealings with Israel. He is quite direct with them as he asks, 'Why did you deceive us ...?' The verb Joshua employs in the question is strong in the

original Hebrew, for it signifies treachery and betrayal. He then pronounces the Gibeonites 'cursed'—that is, they will never be anything but servants to Israel (cf. the similar curse that Noah proclaims for Canaan in Genesis 9:25–27).

Joshua literally says to the Gibeonites in verse 23 that 'there shall not be cut off from you a servant'; the idea of that passage is that not a single Gibeonite will fail to become a servant. The verb 'cut off' is used in an ironic sense here: the same verb occurs five times in Joshua 9 with regard to Gibeon being 'cut into' the covenant. The wordplay is obvious—namely, they have not been 'cut off' from servile duty, even if they have been 'cut into' the covenant.

For the first time we read that the Gibeonites will not only be drawers of water and cutters of wood for the whole congregation, but they will perform the same tasks for 'the house', or tabernacle, of God (9:23). In particular, they will give their service to 'the altar of the LORD' (9:27), which is the bronze altar that stands in the outer courtyard of the tabernacle at the front of the Tent of Meeting (Exodus 27:1–8; 38:1–7). This is the sacrificial altar upon which Israel offers their many whole burnt offerings and sacrifices. To supply wood and water for Israel's extensive sacrificial system would have been an enormous task.

The location of the permanent tabernacle/temple in Canaan is still in doubt. According to verse 27, this will be 'in the place that he should choose'—that is, the location is the Lord's prerogative. The Gibeonites will serve 'the altar' no matter where it is located in Canaan. We know from later texts that the central sanctuary is at Shiloh from the time of Joshua (18:1) until the beginning of the monarchy (1 Samuel 4:3), and after that time it is centred on Jerusalem.

The Gibeonites respond to Joshua by telling the truth (9:24). They own up to their deceitful actions. The Gibeonites had heard that Israel was going to capture 'all' the land and exterminate 'all' its inhabitants; believing the reports, they feared Israel and plotted a plan of guile and treachery—or, as they say, they 'did this thing'. They were simply trying to save their own skins by any means possible. Joshua, in response, keeps his word to them by sparing their lives and making them servants of Israel.

Points to ponder

1. Serving at the altar of the Lord

I recently heard of a large church in the north-eastern United States that hires and pays musicians from outside the church to play during special events, such as services at Christmas Eve and Easter. The principal rationale for doing this is for the church to have a ministry to the large community of musicians in the area. When unbelieving musicians come to play their instruments, they hear the preaching of the gospel. This is perhaps one reason that Joshua chooses the Gibeonites specifically to be cutters of wood and drawers of water 'for the altar of the LORD' (9:27). As servants they will witness the atoning sacrificial system of Israel up close and personally. Their work at the altar may be a redemptive note for the Gibeonites, and it should be understood as a blessing in the midst of cursing (cf. Psalm 84:10).

2. The ever-present danger of self-reliance and pride

One of the reasons that Israel is tricked is because they trusted in themselves rather than in the wisdom of God. Self-reliance, self-will and self-sufficiency are matters of pride, and the people of God must be on constant guard against such things. Martin Luther feared the pope of self above all other popes in

Christendom. Ralph Davis comments that 'Joshua 9 warns God's people against such cocky independence.'[4]

Pride in oneself is a besetting sin in the church, but no more so than in many pastors. The eighteenth-century Puritan William Romaine reflects upon his own pastoral situation when he says:

> O what am I, that such a sinner as I am should be thus highly favoured? A child of wrath by nature, even as others, and by practice, having sinned long with greediness against light and conviction, sinning and sorrowing, sorrowing and sinning, from year to year, a slave to the lust of the flesh, to the lust of the eyes, and to the pride of life, every moment fit and ripe for hell. O what a monument of infinite patience and longsuffering! Spared from day to day, and at last called to the saving knowledge of Jesus.

The people of God today need the attitude and conviction once displayed in the life of the English pastor John Flavel. One Sunday morning Flavel's congregation was waiting for him to come from his study in order to lead the morning worship service. They waited five minutes, and then ten minutes; after fifteen minutes, one of the elders went back to Flavel's study to fetch him for worship. As the elder drew near the study door he overheard Flavel talking and pleading with someone. As he listened, he heard Flavel say, 'I am not going into the pulpit without you'; and he heard Flavel say it over and over again: 'I am not going into the pulpit without you.' When Flavel emerged from the study, he came out alone. But was he really alone?

3. Keeping our word

It is extraordinary and impressive to us today that Israel kept their promises despite the great deceit of the Gibeonites. Would the false claims of the Gibeonites not call into question the validity of the agreement and free the Israelites from having to keep their word? The law of Moses clearly allows an oath to be recalled if it is taken rashly or impulsively (Leviticus 5:4–6). However, oaths that are employed as part of a covenant appear to be of a different class or order, and they must be kept (see Genesis 26:26–31; 2 Samuel 21:7; Ezekiel 16:59–60). And, so, Israel keeps the covenant—and that despite the grumblings of the people.

Our wonder and puzzlement regarding Israel's keeping the covenant with the Gibeonites are partially a reflection of ourselves and of our culture. The reality is that we often hold to a lax view of the given word and take a feeble stance on the truth. Israel is faithful to the covenant made with Gibeon even in its twisted and warped condition. Jesus tells the church that it is better not to make a vow than to fail to keep one that has been made (see Matthew 5:33–37). Even in the midst of our own foolishness, we are to live obediently and faithfully; we are to be true to our word.

13

The battle against the five kings

Please read Joshua 10:1–27

Acentral aspect of the episode before us in this chapter is the power of prayer, and how God cares for his people by answering their prayers in the most mysterious ways. In his old age, George Müller was asked by a reporter how he had kept his orphanages financially afloat during all the many years of his ministry. Müller responded:

No man on earth can say that I ever asked him for a penny. We have no committees, no collectors, no voting and no endowments. All has come in answer to believing prayer. My trust has been in God alone; He has many ways of moving the hearts of men to help us all over the world. While I am praying He speaks to this one and another, on this continent and on that, to send us help. Only the other evening, while I was preaching, a gentleman wrote me a cheque for a large amount for the orphans, and handed it to me when the service was over.

Robert Murray M'Cheyne and Andrew Bonar, two ministers of the Church of Scotland, took an important journey in the 1830s. They were sent by the church to see the state of the Jews in Palestine and the effect that the Presbyterian mission to them was having. They were gone from Scotland for a number of months. M'Cheyne left his church in Dundee in the hands of William Burns, a young evangelist who would one day become a famous missionary to China. There was a great revival in Dundee under Burns' preaching ministry. It is interesting to note that, the very day of the beginning of the revival, there is a statement in M'Cheyne's diary that he had been in prayer all that Sunday for revival in his church. So what were the means of revival in the Dundee church? It was both Burns' preaching and M'Cheyne's praying. In Joshua 10:1-27 we shall see how God answers the prayer of Joshua.

Reaction of the king of Jerusalem (10:1-2)

The peoples of Canaan have reacted in various ways to the Israelite conquests of Jericho and Ai. In Joshua 9:1-2, six people groups mobilized their forces to fight against Israel when they 'heard' of the invasion of their land. The Gibeonites, on the other hand, when they 'heard' of the Israelite attack, sought a covenant of peace with Israel (9:3-27). Now, in chapter 10:1, we read that the king of Jerusalem 'heard' that Israel's army had captured both Jericho and Ai, and that they had devoted both cities to destruction. He also 'heard' that the Gibeonites had sued for peace with Israel and were now in league with them. How will the king of Jerusalem respond to these developments?

Adoni-zedek, king of Jerusalem, is especially distraught over the treaty that the Gibeonites have secured with Israel, and he 'feared greatly'. His dismay stems from the fact that Gibeon, unlike Ai, is a major and powerful city in Canaan. It is 'like one of the royal cities'; this statement may mean that Gibeon has its own king (cf. 1 Samuel 27:5; 2 Samuel 12:26–30) and is at the head of a region of cities (see 9:17 for confirmation of this). Adoni-zedek is also afraid because Gibeon has a well-trained army, yet they have capitulated to the Israelites without a fight.

War against the traitors (10:3–5)

Adoni-zedek summons four other kings who rule either in the highlands of Judah (Hebron) or in the foothills of the Judean mountains (Jarmuth, Lachish, Eglon) to join him. He amasses his coalition in order to attack Gibeon because its inhabitants have made peace with Israel. The Gibeonites are collaborators with the enemy and, therefore, must be punished. Although it is not directly stated in the text, a prime reason for an assault on Gibeon is not merely punitive but didactic; it will serve as a sign to others in Canaan not to do as the Gibeonites have done. It is a warning to the potential traitor.

Major archaeological excavations at Lachish indicate that the city was thriving and at its zenith in the Late Bronze Age—that is, at the time of the Israelite conquest. Excavations in Jerusalem also demonstrate extensive Canaanite/Jebusite building activity. There are also Late Bronze remains at Jarmuth and Hebron, although the extent of the Canaanite occupation has not been adequately defined as yet. The exact location of Eglon is uncertain; some believe it is at the site of modern Tell el-Hesi, which was occupied during the Late Bronze period.

A call to arms (10:6)

The five kings and their armies lay siege to Gibeon, and then they attack the city (10:5). In response, the Gibeonites call on the Israelites for help against the invading forces. An important element of covenant treaties in the ancient Near East is a loyalty, or protection, clause. For example, in a treaty between the Hittite king Mursilis and Duppi-Tessub of Amurru (fourteenth century BC) we read the following clause written by Mursilis:

> If anyone should press you hard, Duppi-Tessub, or [if] anyone should revolt against you, [if] you then write to the king of the Hatti land [Hittites], and the king of the Hatti land dispatches foot soldiers and charioteers to your aid—[if you treat them in an unfair manner], you act in disregard of the gods of the oath.[1]

The Gibeonites here exemplify this element of the covenant treaty: they are petitioning the Israelites to come to their aid in keeping with the covenant promises—one of which is for mutual loyalty and military protection.

Israel's response (10:7–9)

Israel responds immediately to the plea of the Gibeonites. Verse 9 underscores their prompt reaction by declaring that the Israelite troops 'marched up all night from Gilgal', an arduous fifteen-mile uphill trek. The Israelite army arrives in full force: Joshua leads 'all the people of war', and among them are 'all the mighty men of valour'. Thus Israel responds swiftly and vigorously to its covenant commitments to Gibeon.

The Lord encourages Joshua not to fear the armies of the five kings because he has 'given them into your hands'. This divine sanction is the same one that is found in the next chapter of the book, in which the Israelite armies face a coalition of armies from northern Canaan (see 11:6). The command from the Lord that Israel should not be afraid has been a foundational principle of the conquest (Deuteronomy 1:29; 7:21; 20:3; 31:6–8; Joshua 1:9). It is the Lord who fights for Israel and he has already 'given them into your hands'. Indeed, because the Lord leads Israel 'not a man ... shall stand' before Joshua and Israel, a promise that had also been announced earlier by the Lord (Deuteronomy 7:24; 11:25; Joshua 1:5).

The Lord is a man of war (10:10–11)

It needs to be observed that it is God who is at work in Israel's battle against the five kings and their armies. The text says, 'The LORD threw them into a panic' and that literally, *he* 'struck them with a great blow' (10:10); finally, we read that 'the LORD threw down large stones ... on them' (10:11). This is God's war, and he is leading the army of Israel to victory. What Moses had proclaimed of God in Exodus 15:3 is true: 'The LORD is a man of war; the LORD is his name'!

Israel's war against the coalition of five kings contains echoes from the exodus out of Egypt, in which the Lord destroyed Egypt and its army.

First, the statement that 'the LORD threw them into a panic' before Israel is the same language that was used in Exodus 14:24 when God did the same thing to the Egyptian army in the Red Sea.

Secondly, as the armies of the five kings flee before Israel, God casts upon them large 'hailstones' from the sky; more Canaanites are killed by the stones than by the weapons in the hands of the Israelite troops. The humiliation of God's enemies by his striking them with hailstones is reminiscent of the seventh plague upon Egypt (Exodus 9:13–35). In that episode, 'the LORD rained hail upon the land of Egypt ... very heavy hail ... The hail struck down everything that was in the field in all the land of Egypt, both man and beast' (Exodus 9:23–25).

The armies of the coalition flee before, and are pursued by, Israel from Gibeon westward to Beth-horon, and then southward into the Shephelah (= foothills) to the towns of Azekah and Makkedah. The entire distance of the chase is approximately thirty miles. This incursion into the Shephelah opens up the later southern campaign of the Israelite forces (10:29–43).

Sun and moon stand still (10:12–14)

Joshua now prays for God's miraculous intervention in the battle. But what exactly is Joshua praying for in verse 13? The common view is that Joshua asks for an extension of daylight so that the Israelite army could prolong its rout of the five armies of the Canaanite kings. This view receives great support from the final clause of verse 13, which literally says that the sun 'did not hurry to set for an entire day'. Other commentators argue that, in fact, Joshua is asking God to do the opposite of what is usually understood by the verse and lengthen the time of darkness. The command for the sun to 'stand still' is at the heart of the second view; proponents argue that the command does not refer to the sun's movement, but rather to its shining.[2] Support for the lengthening of darkness may be found in the Exodus account. The darkening of the sun in Joshua may echo the ninth plague on Egypt, in which God brings darkness on that land as part of its destruction (Exodus 10:21–29).

The fact that both the sun and the moon 'stand still' in the sky over the grounds of the battle presents an additional difficulty in understanding this episode. Location is important here:

Joshua prays that the sun would stand still 'at Gibeon', which is to the east, and that the moon would do the same to the west over 'Aijalon'. Verse 13 explains that these two celestial bodies 'stood' and 'stopped' in those places until Israel had finished taking vengeance on the Canaanite armies. This scene perhaps recalls the episode of Exodus 14:19-20, when the pillar of cloud stood between the Israelites and the Egyptian army at the Red Sea, and 'one side of the cloud brought light; the other side gave darkness. The Egyptians were clothed in darkness, as they had been during the ninth plague ... But the Hebrews were bathed in the light of the pillar. Symbolically, one represents the children of darkness, and the other the children of light.'[3] It may be that in the episode here in Joshua the Israelites are in the light chasing their enemies into darkness; this scenario not only gives the Israelites a strong military advantage, but may also serve as a metaphor for the sons of light defeating the sons of darkness.

The author of the book of Joshua asks the question, are the words spoken by Joshua in verse 12 not already narrated in the Book of Jameshar? The Book of Jameshar is not extant; it is, however, mentioned on one other occasion in the Old Testament. In 2 Samuel 1:19-27, David utters a poetical lament over the deaths of Saul and Jonathan, a lament that is introduced in verse 18 with the phrase, 'it is written in the Book of Jameshar'. This citation in 2 Samuel has led some scholars to believe that the Book of Jameshar may have been an early collection of Hebrew poetry.

The exceptional nature of the cosmic event at Gibeon is underscored in the phrase, 'There has been no day like it before or since.' The reason given for the wondrous nature of the event, however, is not the miraculous intervention of God in the cosmos, but that 'the LORD obeyed the voice of a man'. In other words, the truly remarkable aspect of the episode is that God answered Joshua's prayer in such a timely manner! The real miracle in this story is the miracle of prayer. As Ralph Davis comments, 'That day was unique not for some unusual daylight or darkness but because Yahweh listened to a man's prayer!'[4] The truth is that, as Robert Murray M'Cheyne put it, 'A man is what he is on his knees before God, and nothing more.' Joshua and the Israelites prevail at Gibeon only because of God's answer to prayer. Prayer can move mountains and stop the movements of the sun and the moon.

In 1932 D. Martyn Lloyd-Jones was on an extended visit to the United States. He was engaged at short notice to speak at the Chautauqua Conference Center. He had not planned on going there, but, at the last minute, one of speakers became ill and Lloyd-Jones was hurriedly put in his place. The arrangement was that he would preach for a week, starting on Monday and ending on Friday. Over the years the conference had become secularized, but there were a few Christians who continued to pray for better things to come for it. On Monday, 11 July, some thirty people came to hear Lloyd-Jones (although there were thousands attending the conference). By Friday, Lloyd-Jones' final service was moved to the concert hall that held 6,000 people, and the place was jammed full. Oh, the power of prayer!

Flight of the five kings (10:16–18)

In the light of the ongoing rout of their armies, the five Amorite/Canaanite kings flee for their lives. They run to the area of the town of Makkedah, approximately thirty miles from Gibeon, and hide in a cave. Advancing Israelite troops discover that the five kings are sequestered in a cave, and so they report their find to Joshua. Joshua, however, does not want to halt the continuously raging battle to reckon with the pagan kings. So he commands his troops to use large boulders to seal the opening to the cave and to place a military guard outside it. The kings' hideout becomes a prison as they await inescapable judgement.

Utter defeat (10:19–21)

Joshua had prayed, and the sun 'stood still' (10:13); now, in contrast, Joshua commands his troops, literally, 'But you, you do not stand still' (10:19). The Israelite forces are to pursue the enemy troops and, literally, 'cut them off at the tail'. That same expression is used in Deuteronomy 25:18 regarding the way that the Amalekites waged war on Israel in the wilderness. It is an idiom for an attack on the rearguard. In addition, the Israelite army is to prevent the enemy forces from entering their own 'fortified cities' where they cannot be easily dislodged (10:20). Although a remnant of survivors escape the battle to find refuge in their fortified cities, the Hebrew troops inflict utter defeat on the Amorite armies.

The Israelite army then returns to the military encampment at Makkedah. The soldiers return 'safe' to the camp and with a triumphant victory. Verse 21 relays one major result of the Israelite conquest: the text literally says, 'No man sharpened his tongue against the sons of Israel.' The expression 'sharpen the tongue' is found in the book of Exodus during the final plague on Egypt (Exodus 11:7). It 'signifies angry growling'.[5] Perhaps this means that no pagan spoke in opposition to the people of God. After Israel's great defeat of the armies of the five kings, hostility against them from the peoples of the highlands is silenced.

Return to the imprisoned kings (10:22–27)

The location of the cave in which the five kings are incarcerated lies in the general area of the Israelite encampment at Makkedah (10:16). Joshua commands his men to remove the boulders from the entrance to the cave and to bring the five kings in front of him. He then summons all of his soldiers to witness how he will judge the kings (10:24).

Joshua calls his military commanders to come forward and he charges them to place their feet on the necks of the five kings. This is a symbolic act to reflect the ideas of authority and subjugation. It is similar to the figure of an enemy as the 'footstool' under his conqueror's feet (see Psalm 110:1). Joshua also employs this act by the victors as a symbol of the future: this is what God will do to other enemies who are left in the land of promise—they too will submit (10:25).

Joshua executes the five kings and then hangs them on five trees. They are hung, not as a method of execution, but rather as a public display of the criminal and his end. It is a sign of curse and humiliation (Deuteronomy 21:22–23), 'and it may have acted as a deterrent against such criminal behaviour. In regard to the latter purpose, the practice in medieval England of impaling the heads of notorious criminals on London Bridge may be an equivalent from more recent times'.[6] And, just like the episode dealing with the king of Ai, these five kings are hung on trees only until evening (8:29; 10:26). The Torah commands that the body of a criminal shall 'not remain all night on the tree, but you shall bury him the same day' (Deuteronomy 21:23). In accordance with Torah law, the Israelites bury the five kings that day in the cave in Makkedah where they had originally hidden (10:27).

The burial is completed when the Israelites roll huge boulders in front of the cave to seal it. The concluding statement that it is there 'to this very day' indicates that the site serves as a stone monument (see 7:26; 8:28–29). This is the fifth stone monument set up by the Israelites after they entered the land of promise

(4:20; 7:26; 8:28–29; 8:30–32). They must not forget the great deeds of God in their midst.

Points to ponder

God works mightily through the prayers of his people
In the episode at Gibeon the Lord answered the prayer of Joshua in a mighty way. God still works great things through the prayers of his people today. Prayer is a primary instrument of God's work. E. M. Bounds begins his book *Power Through Prayer* in the following manner:

> We are constantly on a stretch, if not on a strain, to devise new methods, new plans, new organizations to advance the church and secure enlargement and efficiency for the gospel. The trend of the day has a tendency to lose sight of the man or sink the man in the plan or organization. God's plan is to make much of the man, far more of him than anything else. Men are God's great method. The church is looking for better methods; God is looking for better men... What the church needs today is not more machinery, or better, not new organizations or more and novel methods, but men whom the Holy Spirit can use, men of prayer, men mighty in prayer. The Holy Spirit does not flow through methods, but through men, He does not come on machinery, but on men. He does not anoint plans, but men—men of prayer.[7]

14

The southern campaign

Please read Joshua 10:28–43

After Israel defeats the five Amorite kings, the Israelite forces under the command of Joshua take the opportunity to inflict further defeat on the inhabitants of Canaan. The army sweeps through the southern foothills and the southern highlands, subduing six important Canaanite towns. Modern scholarship calls this invasion during the conquest of Canaan Joshua's 'southern campaign'.

God is the one leading Israel in battle: this theme drives the biblical narrative of the southern campaign. It is the Lord who commands Israel to conquer this land (10:40-41); he is the one who gives the cities into the hands of Israel's army (10:30,32); he is the one who equips Israel for war, and he fights on their behalf (10:42). God's work alone causes Israel to triumph in this campaign. The church throughout history is conquering because of the Lord's leading.

John Newton wrote the following to William Wilberforce's wife:

> Though we are poor, He is rich; though we are weak, He is strong; though we have nothing, He possesses all things … He conquered in his own person, and He will make each of his members more than conquerors in due season … He can control all that we fear; so that if our paths should be through fire or through water, neither the flood shall drown us, nor the flame kindle upon us.

Beginning of the southern campaign (10:28–32)

The army of Israel is encamped near the town of Makkedah (10:21), the same location where Joshua executed the five Amorite kings and sealed their bodies within a cave (10:22–27). The town itself, however, remains in Canaanite control. So Joshua captures Makkedah and kills every person in the city, including its king, just as he had done in Jericho (6:21). The treatment of Makkedah by the Israelites sets a pattern for how they deal with the remaining five towns of the southern campaign: Libnah (10:29–30), Lachish (10:31–32), Eglon (10:34–35), Hebron (10:36–37) and Debir (10:38–39). There are some variations in the pattern for each city, and these reflect the peculiarities and particularities of each battle.

With regard to the battle at Libnah, the text does not say that Israel 'captured' the city, as it does for the other cities (cf. 10:28). They do, however, invoke and apply the ban on its inhabitants; all humans in Libnah, including its king, are slaughtered. One addition to the pattern is the recognition that 'the LORD'—that is, Yahweh—is the one who gives Libnah and Lachish into Israelite hands; that comment was not made with reference to the assault on Makkedah.

Lachish is the third city attacked by Israel, and its defence is more formidable than that of the two previous cities. Israel is forced to lay siege to Lachish, but it is soon captured, 'on the second day'. The king of Lachish is not mentioned; he has already been killed by Joshua and his corpse sealed in a cave at Makkedah (10:23,27).

Horam intervenes (10:33)

The pattern of conquest is interrupted by this verse, which describes the intervention of Horam, king of Gezer, on behalf of the city of Lachish. The town of Gezer is located in the Shephelah, approximately twenty miles north of Lachish. Apparently the Israelite army totally annihilates the Gezerite forces, leaving none remaining. There is, however, no mention in the text of the capture of Gezer. It does not become an Israelite possession until Pharaoh gives it to Solomon as a dowry for the marriage of his daughter to the Israelite king (1 Kings 9:15-17).

More conquered towns (10:34-39)

The pattern of conquest now resumes as the Israelite army marches from Lachish to Eglon. If Eglon is correctly identified with the modern site of Tell el-Hesi, then it lies approximately five miles to the south-west of Lachish in the Shephelah. Joshua captures Eglon and destroys all the people in it, but no king is mentioned because he also was killed earlier and entombed in a cave at Makkedah (10:23,27).

The forces of Joshua then 'went up' from Eglon to Hebron (10:36). Eglon lies next to the coastal plain, so that traversing the land from Eglon to Hebron is an uphill journey into the Judaean highlands. Hebron lies approximately 3,000 feet (or 900 metres) above sea level. The Israelites capture Hebron and destroy all its inhabitants and 'its king and its towns'. The king of Hebron was among the kings executed at Makkedah earlier in the chapter (10:23) and, thus, the ruler mentioned here is his successor. The addition of 'its towns' to the list of those struck by Israel indicates that Hebron stands as the main city of a regional kingdom. Israel, therefore, conquers not only Hebron, but the entire region under Hebron's rule.

After the defeat of the Hebron region, Israel's forces 'turned back' to attack the city of Debir. Debir is probably located at the modern site of Khirbet Rabud, a large city during the period of the conquest. It lies approximately five miles south-west of Hebron. By striking in that direction, the army of Israel is 'turning back' towards the Shephelah, from which they had come in their attack on Hebron. The pattern of the conquest of Debir is almost exactly the same as that of the attack on Hebron.

Total conquest (10:40–43)

These verses summarize the extent of Israel's military campaign thus far in Canaan. The four points of the compass mark the amount of territory captured in the conquest; the Israelites have secured the land extending from Kadesh-barnea in the south, located in the Negeb, as far as Gibeon in the north, located six miles north-west of Jerusalem in the Judaean highlands. It also extends from Gaza in the west along the Mediterranean Sea, as far as the land of Goshen in the east, located in Transjordan. Note well that the northernmost land is Gibeon; it is not until chapter 11 that much of the land north of Gibeon is conquered.

The biblical narrative seems to imply that all of this land has been conquered and is in the possession of Israel (10:42). Yet how is this passage to be reconciled with later statements in the books of Joshua and Judges (see 13:1–6; Judges 1) that appear to contradict it by reflecting a conquest that was not fully achieved? According to verse 43, at the close of the central and southern campaigns Israel returns to its camp at Gilgal. The text gives no indication that Israel leaves occupying forces in the areas they conquered. Therefore, it is quite possible that the indigenous Canaanites subsequently repopulate the cities subdued by Israel in the highlands and Shephelah.

The phrase 'at one time' found in verse 42 lends support to this idea. According to a study by Jeffrey Niehaus, this phrase can be used idiomatically to mean that Joshua and his troops had once conquered the land, but they did not remain in control of it. Niehaus suggests that this could signify that 'later battles were required to retake certain locales'.[1] Such a reconstruction would make sense of the various tribal wars in these areas related in the book of Judges.

Points to ponder

1. The Christian life is a battle

The text tells us that Israel triumphed 'because the LORD God of Israel fought for Israel'. The same is true for the people of God throughout the ages; the church is triumphant because of the triumph of Christ! Yet the fact that God fights for his people does not excuse the people of God from going forth to battle and putting up the good fight of the faith. The Christian life and walk are warfare.

From pulpits today, many pastors commonly teach that Christians ought to seek a life of comfort, ease and prosperity. The idea of the prosperity gospel is that God promises Christians calm seas on their pilgrimage through life. And, moreover, because God fights for his people, then they ought to have expectations of comfort—and, indeed, one ought to seek the comfortable pilgrimage. But is this really true? Is this the proper understanding of the Christian life?

Isaac Watts asks this very question in his hymn, 'Am I a Soldier of the Cross?' In the second stanza he says:

Must I be carried to the skies
on flowery beds of ease,
while others fought to win the prize,
and sailed through bloody seas?

Isn't the reality that God does not promise his people calm seas, but only that they will reach port safely? He does not promise us a wealthy, prosperous, easy, comfortable pilgrimage; he only gives his word that we shall arrive safely. The truth is that many believers go through the crucible of life, through the spiritual wars, and the question is: how will believers respond to the fiery ordeal and the raging war?

2. We are called to be good soldiers for Christ

R. C. Sproul often tells the story of a young Greek man who was eager to fight in a great battle. He was underage, so he decided to sneak away from home to join the troops in the field. He successfully joined the army but, as the battle began, a great fear overcame him. He had not expected war to be like this. In his fear, he ran from the field.

His commanding officer sent soldiers to find him and bring him back. When he was found he was taken before the king. The king demanded to know his name. Ashamed, the young man only mumbled a response.

As the king grew angrier, he demanded, 'Young man, what is your name?'

The young man answered, 'Alexander, your Majesty.'

With that response King Alexander the Great shouted at the frightened young man, 'Alexander? Young man, either change your name or change your behaviour!'

Do we bear the name 'Christian'? If so, do we fight for Christ our King? Do we soldier in the name of Jesus? If not, then we must either change our name or change our behaviour!

15

The northern campaign

Please read Joshua 11:1–23

One of the major theological teachings of the conquest narrative is that the entire affair is unfolding according to the counsel and plan of God. The sovereignty of God is the very foundation of the Israelite conquest; it is his will that is at work in this event. A. W. Pink says that:

> The sovereignty of God may be defined as the exercise of His supremacy ... God does as He pleases, only as He pleases, always as He pleases ... Divine sovereignty means that God in fact, as well as in name, that He is on the throne of the universe directing all things, working all things 'after the counsel of His own will' (Ephesians 1:11).[1]

We read in verse 20 of Joshua chapter 11 that the Canaanites fought against Israel because 'it was the LORD's doing to harden their hearts that they should come against Israel in battle'. How are we to understand this grand theological statement? John Calvin supplies the answer when he says:

> Hence we maintain that by his providence, not heaven and earth and inanimate creatures only, but also the counsels and wills of men are so governed as to move exactly in the course which he has destined. What, then, will you say, does nothing happen fortuitously, nothing contingently? I answer, it was a true saying of Basil the Great, that fortune and chance are heathen terms, the meaning of which ought not to occupy pious minds. For if all success is blessing from God, and calamity and adversity are his curse, there is no place left in human affairs for fortune and chance. [2]

In addition, it ought to be understood that God is not causing the Canaanites to despise and resist Israel. Indeed not! They do that of their own accord. But what God is doing is giving them over to their own desires and leaving them to carry out their own evil schemes (see Romans 1). He does not change their hearts, but allows them to act according to their own hearts.

A northern coalition (11:1–5)

Hazor was a major site in Canaan during the period of the conquest. It was located at the modern site of Tell el-Qedah, which lies eight and a half miles north of the Sea of Galilee. At this period the city was at its peak materially: it covered an area of 200 acres and was the largest city in Canaan at the time. Hazor is well known from extra-biblical texts of the second millennium BC, including the Egyptian Execration Texts (nineteenth to eighteenth centuries BC), the Mari Texts (eighteenth century BC), and the Egyptian Amarna Letters (fourteenth century BC). It is clear from these documents that

Hazor was a major commercial centre in the ancient Near East prior to Israel's conquest of the land.

The name of Hazor's king is Jabin. This is not the same Jabin that is mentioned in Judges 4; the Jabin in this episode is killed by Joshua in verse 10 of the present chapter. We know that Jabin was a dynastic name, for it is used of the rulers of Hazor in both the Mari Texts and the Amarna Letters.

In any event, the contemporary Jabin responds to Israel's conquests in the south by building a military coalition of Canaanite kings to make war against Israel. This confederation includes soldiers from a broad geographical spectrum in the north: from the Samarian highlands and foothills to Dor along the Mediterranean Coast, and to the foot of Mount Hermon in the far north. This coalition constitutes 'a great horde ... like the sand that is on the seashore' (11:4). The latter clause is an idiom for a huge number; it is hyperbole (see Genesis 22:17; 32:12; Judges 7:12). In addition, the force is also formidable because of a large presence of cavalry and chariotry. This army is a threat to Israel, perhaps the greatest danger they have faced thus far.

The confederate forces then gather and encamp at 'the waters of Merom'. The location of Merom is uncertain. The site is mentioned, however, in some extra-biblical ancient Near-Eastern texts, most notably, in the military itineraries of Pharaoh Thutmosis III (fifteenth century BC) and the Assyrian King Tiglath-pileser III (eighth century BC). It must, therefore, be a place of strategic value.

The battle of Merom (11:6–9)
This massive enemy presence could certainly cause Israel to respond in dread and awe; it is 'a great horde' prepared for

battle. The Lord, however, commands Joshua: 'Do not be afraid of them.' This charge is a key theme that echoes throughout the book of Joshua when Israel is facing a daunting military situation (1:9; 8:1; 10:25). And the reason Israel is to have no fear is because God is acting in, and controlling, the event. He promises, 'I will give over all of them, slain, to Israel' (11:6).

Joshua and his men are to act as well. After victory is secured for the Israelite army, they are to 'hamstring' the enemy's horses and 'burn their chariots' (11:6). Both of these actions are preventive, so that the cavalry and these chariots would not be used against them again. These two forces give the Canaanites a distinct advantage over the Israelite army, which consists mainly of foot soldiers.

The Israelite forces then spring a surprise attack on the Canaanite coalition. The Hebrew word for 'suddenly' (11:7) bears the idea of an invasion that happens swiftly and surprisingly (cf. Isaiah 47:11; 48:3; Jeremiah 4:20). The unexpected sweep of the attack helps to render the cavalry and chariotry useless because it takes time to prepare those forces for battle. The Canaanite army responds by fleeing the field, and the Israelites pursue them all the way to the Valley of Mizpeh. This is the northernmost point of the land belonging to the Canaanite kings of the coalition (11:3). Joshua's forces simply sweep the land of them.

Hazor (11:10–11)

The Israelite army returns from the north, and they attack and capture the city of Hazor. The king of Hazor had been the dominant force in establishing the northern confederation to resist Israel and, as the text points out, it 'was the head of all those kingdoms' (11:10). Like lopping off the head of a dangerous snake, Joshua destroys the head of the enemy coalition. After Hazor's capture, Joshua places every living thing under the *cherem*, or ban, so that everything that has life is destroyed. The Israelites then burn the city.

Archaeological work at Hazor has revealed several major destruction levels at the site: two of these occurred at the end of the fifteenth century BC and in the second half of the thirteenth century BC. Archaeologists differ regarding which conflagration was perpetrated by the Israelite army under the direction of Joshua.

All the cities of the north (11:12–15)

After the destruction of Hazor, Joshua and his men turn to deal with the other kings and cities of the Canaanite confederation. The Israelites capture all of them, and they implement a partial ban on the cities by killing every human within them (11:11). This is not a fully-fledged *cherem* because Israel keeps the spoil and plunder for themselves (11:14). In addition, the Israelite forces do not burn these cities to the ground as they did to Hazor. Hazor is the only site torched during the northern campaign. They did, however, burn the cities of Jericho and Ai in the earlier central campaign (6:24; 8:28).

The Israelites are not to destroy every city in their path; they merely plunder many of them. This is done according to the Word of God spoken to Moses prior to the conquest. The Lord had said:

And when the LORD your God brings you into the land that he swore to your fathers, to Abraham, to Isaac, and to Jacob, to give you—with great and good cities that you did not build, and houses full of all good things that you did not fill, and cisterns that you did not dig, and vineyards and olive trees that you did not plant ... (Deuteronomy 6:10–11).

In this matter, the text tells us that Joshua does not falter or disobey; he does not reject a word from God's commands (11:15).

The initial conquest of the land (11:16–18)

In Joshua 10:40–43, the biblical author had summarized the area and extent of the conquest up to that point in time. That report did not include the northern campaign. Now we read a further summary that includes the northern campaign, and the writer concludes that Joshua captured 'all that land'—that is, Canaan and parts of Transjordan (11:16–17).

A couple of things need to be noted about this initial conquest of the land.

First of all, the capture of the land is not lightning fast—a *blitzkrieg*—as is often supposed. Verse 18 makes clear that Joshua fought with the kings of the land for 'a long time'. How long does this initial conquest take? Scholars calculate it by the chronology of the life of Caleb. Caleb was forty years old when he was sent by Moses from Kadesh-barnea to spy out the land of Canaan (14:7). Because of the evil report of most of the spies (Numbers 13–14) the Israelites are made to wander in the wilderness an additional thirty-eight years (Deuteronomy 2:14). Caleb is, therefore, seventy-eight years old when the conquest of Canaan begins. He then receives his land allotment at Hebron when he is eighty-five years old (14:10). Thus the initial conquest of the land takes approximately seven years to complete.

Secondly, it is important to understand that the general conquest of the land does not mean a full occupation of it.

The reality is that Israel does not dispossess all the peoples of Canaan (see 17:11–13; Judges 1:17–33). So, for instance, although the Israelites destroy the city of Hazor with fire, it is soon reoccupied by Canaanites (see Judges 4:17,23–24).

The sovereignty of God (11:19–20)

The conquest of Canaan is an all-out war between Israel and the inhabitants of the land. There is only one exception: the Gibeonites deceived the Israelites into a covenant that spared them from being vanquished by Israel (9:1–27). The Hebrew forces captured the rest of 'them all in battle' (11:19). The reason that there is such an extensive and wholesale conflict is directly stated in the text: 'it was the LORD's doing' (11:20). It was from the Lord, literally, 'to harden their heart' so that they would engage Israel in battle.

The motif of God hardening the heart of Israel's enemies is first found in the events leading up to the exodus from Egypt. In Exodus 4:21, God says about Pharaoh, 'I will harden his heart.' The Lord hardens Pharaoh's heart to demonstrate that only the God of the Hebrews is the Sovereign of the universe. The idea that the Lord controls even Pharaoh's heart is one of the main points of the Exodus conflict. 'In addition, the fact that this passage is prophetic reflects divine dominion over the unfolding of history.'[3] That same word for 'harden' is used in the present passage from Joshua, and here it bears the same meaning as in the account of the Exodus—which is that God is in total control of the situation and outcome of the Israelite conquest.

The Anakim (11:21–22)

In the final act of Joshua's initial campaigns to capture the land of Canaan, his troops clear the highlands of a people group called the Anakim. When the Israelites first came to the borders of Canaan during the wilderness wanderings, Moses sent spies to 'go up into the hill country, and see what the land is, and whether the people who dwell in it are strong or weak, whether they are few or many ...' (Numbers 13:17–18). The spies scouted the highlands and they returned with a warning: '... all the people that we saw in it are of great height. And there we saw the Nephilim (the sons of Anak, who come from the Nephilim), and we seemed to ourselves like grasshoppers, and so we seemed to them' (Numbers 13:32–33). There was great fear on the part of Israel to attack Canaan at that time. But now, at the close of the conquest, Israel summarily cuts off the Anakim from the highlands and utterly destroys their cities. No Anakim are left in the hill country, but they remain in the Plain of Philistia in three capital cities of the Philistines—Gaza, Gath and Ashdod. Later there is a giant race among the Philistines in Gath during David's days (1 Samuel 17:4; 2 Samuel 21:15–22).

Consequently, those whom Israel feared most in the land are the last ones to be conquered during the initial military campaigns. And the Anakim are done away with in a cursory fashion, almost as an afterthought to the major military fighting. They prove not to be a great threat after all—the peril was really in the minds of the spies, and they truly exaggerated the danger. Giant people are as nothing before the Holy One of Israel!

Summary and transition (11:23)
This concluding verse of the chapter serves two purposes.

First, it sums up all the narrative material beginning with Joshua 5:13 to this point: Joshua has generally captured all the land of Canaan and so, for a time, Canaan will lie undisturbed by war. God commanded Israel through Moses to capture the land (Numbers 34:1-12), and under Joshua's leadership they succeeded.

Secondly, this verse is also transitional because it anticipates the allocation of the land to the twelve tribes by Joshua in chapters 13-19.

Points to ponder

God is sovereign over all the affairs of men

In this passage we see that the Lord controlled even the hearts of the Canaanites that they would resist Israel and make battle against them. One aspect of the doctrine of sovereignty is that God controls and directs all the deeds of men.

> Solomon observes that 'the heart of man plans his way, but the LORD establishes his steps' (Proverbs 16:9), and 'man's steps are from the LORD; how then can man understand his way?' (Proverbs 20:24). The psalmist agrees, stating, 'The LORD brings the counsel of the nations to nothing; he frustrates the plans of the peoples. The counsel of the LORD stands for ever, the plans of his heart to all generations' (Psalm 33:10-11). Observe, especially, the words of the Book of Daniel: 'for his dominion is an everlasting dominion, and his kingdom endures from generation to generation; all the inhabitants of the earth are accounted as nothing, and he does according to his will among the host of heaven and among the inhabitants of the earth; and none can stay his hand or say to him, "What have you done?"' (Daniel 4:34-35).[4]

E. B. Pusey reminds us that everything unfolds according to the will and plan of God. He says:

This, then, is of faith, that everything, the very least, or what seems to us great, every change of the seasons, everything which touches us in mind, body, or estate, whether brought about through this outward senseless nature, or by the will of man, good or bad, is overruled to each of us by the all-holy and all-loving will of God. Whatever befalls us, however it befalls us, we must receive as the will of God. If it befalls us through man's negligence, or ill-will, or anger, still it is, in even the least circumstance, to us the will of God. For if the least thing could happen to us without God's permission, it would be something out of God's control. God's providence or his love would not be what they are. Almighty God himself would not be the same God; not the God whom we believe, adore, and love.[5]

16

Summary of the conquest

Please read Joshua 12:1–24

Chapter 12 of Joshua concludes a long narrative of the conquest of the land of Canaan by the military forces of Israel (5:13–12:24). The purpose of this chapter is to demonstrate that God has fulfilled his promise to give the land of Canaan to his covenant people. This promise was made as early as Genesis 12:7, in which 'the LORD appeared to Abram and said, "To your offspring I will give this land."' That initial promise was made at least five hundred years before the conquest under Joshua. William Gurnall comments on this length of time:

> God's promises are dated, but with a mysterious character; and, for want of skill in God's chronology, we are prone to think God forgets us, when, indeed, we forget ourselves in being so bold as to set God a time of our own, and in being angry that he comes not just then to us.

God's promise to Abraham that Canaan would belong to his descendants is clearly according to the Lord's own plan and timing!

The promise of God that Israel would inherit the land of Canaan was repeated by him numerous times after the initial pledge to Abraham (see Genesis 15:18; 24:7; 26:4; 35:12; Numbers 34:2; Deuteronomy 34:4). And so, finally, after the patriarchal period, 400 years in slavery and forty years of wandering in the wilderness, the people of Israel realize the fulfilment of God's oath to them that they would gain entrance to, and control, the land of Canaan.

East of the Jordan River (12:1)

The first six verses of this chapter summarize the Israelite conquest and capture of areas in Transjordan. The text refers to these lands as 'beyond the Jordan', which reflects the viewpoint of the writer, who is in the land of promise. The primary purpose of this overview is to underscore the fact that the Transjordanian possession is part of Israel's inheritance. The tribes of Reuben, Gad and the half-tribe of Manasseh that are settling there are neither outcasts nor second-class citizens; the writer's concern is 'to stress the unity of all Israel'.[1]

The author then provides a general description of the land that Israel seized in Transjordan. The southern border is 'the Valley of the Arnon', or the Arnon River.[2] This was the southern boundary of the territory of King Sihon (Deuteronomy 2:24,36). The northern border of Israelite occupation is Mount Hermon (Deuteronomy 3:8–10). Boundary lines to the east are less well-defined, simply being construed as the 'Arabah', or desert lands to the east.

Sihon's kingdom (12:2–3)

These two verses provide greater detail concerning the land that was captured by Israel during the Transjordanian conquest. The dispossession of Sihon, king of the Amorites, is recorded in Numbers 21:21–32. Sihon had refused to allow Israel passage through his territory, and so Israel attacked his army, defeated it and took possession of the land. Sihon's land extended from the Arnon River in the south to the Jabbok River in the north, and it was bounded by the desert lands to the east. The tribes of Reuben and Gad occupy and settle these lands that formerly belonged to Sihon.

Og's kingdom (12:4–5)

Israel's conquest of the territory of Og, king of Bashan, is recorded in Numbers 21:33–35. From the Jabbok River, the Israelites thrust northward into the region of Bashan. This is a land noted for its lushness and fertility (Amos 4:1). Og responded by mustering his army and meeting Israel in battle at Edrei. Israel defeated the Bashanites and took possession of their land. The half-tribe of Manasseh settles in this area.

Leadership (12:6)

The final verse of the passage relating to the Transjordan places emphasis on the leadership of Moses as he commands the army of Israel under the direction of the Lord. He is twice referred to as 'the servant of the LORD'. When Moses leads the capture of Transjordanian land and gives possession of it to the two and a half tribes, he is doing so with God's blessing and sanction. This fact adds legitimacy to the claim of those tribes that they are rightfully settling in those areas.

West of the Jordan River (12:7–8)

The author now summarizes the conquest of the land and kings on 'the west side of the Jordan' under the leadership of Joshua. Moses was forbidden to enter the land of Canaan, and his mantle of leadership was bestowed on Joshua. The deeds of both men with regard to conquest are here set in parallel.

As with the description of the conquest of Transjordan (12:1), the author provides a very broad sketch of the land acquired under Joshua's leadership. It extends from 'Baal-gad in the Valley of Lebanon to Mount Halak, that rises towards Seir' in the south (12:7; cf. 11:17). The precise location of Baal-gad is unknown, although the Valley of Lebanon in which it lies is situated between two mountain ranges, the Lebanon and the anti-Lebanon. This is to the north of the city of Daniel The exact location of Mount Halak is also uncertain; the text simply tells us that it 'rises towards Seir'; Seir is a general designation for the land of Edom (Numbers 24:18). Therefore, Mount Halak lies in the general region of the Arabah to the south of the Dead Sea.

Verse 8 provides more specifics concerning the land conquered by the Israelites on the west side of the Jordan River. The subjugated territory includes the highlands, the Shephelah, the Arabah, the slopes, the desert and the Negeb—this is a basic repetition of Joshua 10:40, which says that Joshua 'struck the whole land'. In order that the reader might be impressed with the broad extent of the conquest, the author enumerates the various peoples that Israel pummelled; this is a recurring feature of the conquest narratives (Deuteronomy 7:1; Joshua 3:10; 11:3).

A list of kings (12:9–24)
After having reviewed the general geographical extent of the conquest and the affected people groups, the author now provides a list of kings defeated by the Israelite army on the west side of the Jordan. The list roughly follows the order of

the conquest given in the previous narrative of Joshua (5:13–11:23). It has the appearance of an ancient Near-Eastern military catalogue or itinerary. Thutmosis III (*c.* 1479–1425 BC), for example, began the custom in Egypt of providing campaign journals that give a roster of cities that he had conquered, or over which he claimed dominion. Subsequent pharaohs followed his lead: Amenophis II (*c.* 1427–1401 BC), Sethos I (*c.* 1306–1290 BC), and Shishak (*c.* 945–924 BC).[3] This section of Joshua fits well into that genre.

The list adds the names of some cities that are not mentioned in the narrative texts of Joshua, such as Taanach and Megiddo. This demonstrates that the conquest narratives are selective in the victories that they report. The total number of kings (and their cities) defeated by the Israelites comes to thirty-one.

Points to ponder

1. God keeps his promises

It should be encouraging to believers that God keeps his promises to his people despite their outward circumstances. In 1662, Richard Baxter was thrown out of his pulpit and church as a result of the Act of Uniformity. This was the 'Great Ejectment' when hundreds of Puritans were tossed out of their pulpits because they would not agree to the demands of the Church of England. Baxter's response was simple and direct: 'Never did God break His promise to me. Never did He fail me or forsake me. *The sun may cease to shine on man, and the earth to bear us, but God will never cease to be faithful to His promise.*' Baxter's confidence was never shaken in the midst of such persecution and darkness.

Like Baxter, our confidence as Christians should never wax

and wane because of adverse circumstances. In one of his last sermons, the nineteenth-century Scots pastor Alexander Somerville declared the following:

> No power of king, emperor or czar, of police, or pope or spiritual potentate; not the madness of scepticism or superstition, of atheism or heathenism; not all the resources of the prince of the power of the air, are able to hold the ground before the Lord Jesus, acting through the sympathy, faith and prayers of His people. For my part, were I not now nearing the close of my life, I should go forward with more confidence than ever, today, in Christ's unrestricted promise, *if ye have faith, nothing shall be impossible for you.*

2. God's plans are accomplished in his time

God's promise to Israel that they would possess the land of Canaan took over 500 years to come to pass. We should be reminded that God accomplishes his plans in his own way and according to his own timing. That means that Christians ought to be patient. How frequently the Scriptures tell us to 'wait for the LORD'! (Psalm 27:14; 130:5; Isaiah 40:31). That is difficult in a world that is so fast-paced, and one that demands instant success and gratification. But the Lord does not act according to our timetables. A. J. Gordon, in his book *The Holy Spirit in Missions*, tells believers to persevere and wait on Jesus:

> It was seven years before Carey baptized his first convert in India. It was seven years before Judson won his first disciple in Burma. Morrison toiled seven years before the first Chinese were brought to Christ. Moffat declared that he waited seven years to see the first evident moving of the Holy Spirit upon his Bechuanas of Africa. Henry Richards

laboured seven years on the Congo before the first convert was gained at Banza Manteka.

We ought to ask ourselves, have we ever waited seven years for anything?

Part 3:

The dividing (13:1–21:45)

17

Distribution of the land
east of the Jordan

Please read Joshua 13:1–33

T his chapter begins the third major section of the book of Joshua. The opening chapters of the book narrate the crossing of Israel into the land of promise (1:1–5:12), and the second part presents a generally completed conquest of Canaan (5:13–12:24). This third part details the assignment of the land to the various tribes (13:1–21:45). What a great event! God promised as early as Genesis 12 that this territory would be deeded to Israel; he said to Abraham, 'To your offspring I will give this land' (v. 7). And the Lord repeated that promise again and again to the Hebrews (see, for example, Genesis 13:15; 17:8; Exodus 33:1; Numbers 32:11). Here at last their wanderings are over; here at last God fulfils his promise; here at last Israel tastes the sweetness of the land of promise; here they are finally home!

For the modern reader who is working through the allocation of the land, chapter after chapter, it can be quite daunting and tedious. We need to remember, however, what a welcome and joyous event this was in the life of the people of the covenant. The joy of the Israelite in his land inheritance is reflected throughout the Old Testament; it simply resounds in passage after passage. For example, we read in Psalm 16:

> As for the saints in the land, they are the excellent ones,
>   in whom is all my delight.
> The LORD is my chosen portion and my cup;
>   you hold my lot.
> The lines have fallen for me in pleasant places;
>   indeed, I have a beautiful inheritance
>
> (Psalm 16:3,5–6).

The Lord's command to apportion the land (13:1–7)

This third major section of the book of Joshua begins in much the same way as the first one did, with both the Lord and the writer proclaiming the status of Israel's covenant mediator. In 1:1–2 they both announce that Moses is dead, and in 13:1 they both report that Joshua is 'old and advanced in years'. The standing of the two men at the close of life serves as an indicator that a new, major event or episode is about to unfold: Moses' death is followed by the important story of the conquest; Joshua's old age is followed by the deeding of the conquered land to the twelve tribes of Israel.

The Lord then gives consideration to the status of the previously conquered land (13:2–6). Although the Israelites succeeded in the military conquest of Canaan, some regions were not subjugated or settled. The areas listed here are still in play, and they are primarily located in the coastal areas of

Canaan, of Phoenicia and of the very northern limits of the land of promise. What we are witnessing is the fluctuation and movements of people groups: for instance, the Philistines are in the process of becoming entrenched in the coastal plains, and the Canaanites are resettling areas that had been captured by the Israelites. The occupation of Canaan by the Israelites is anything but static, nor should one expect it to be. Despite the constant shifting of people groups in Canaan, the Lord orders Joshua to divide the land and allocate it to the tribes of Israel (13:6–7). He is to apportion it 'to the nine tribes and half the tribe of Manasseh'. But before that allotment is deeded the author of Joshua reviews the tribal inheritance on the east side of the Jordan that belongs to the Reubenites, Gadites and the half-tribe of Manasseh.

General disposition of the eastern lands (13:8–14)

Moses has already distributed the land east of the Jordan to the Reubenites, Gadites and the half-tribe of Manasseh (Numbers 32:33; Deuteronomy 3:12–13). Verse 8 emphasizes the fact that Moses partitioned the eastern lands to these tribes as it twice says, 'Moses gave them'. However, the partitioning agreement required the Reubenites, Gadites and the half-tribe of Manasseh to take up arms and help the other tribes secure their inheritance on the west side of the Jordan. Only then would Reuben, Gad and the half-tribe of Manasseh fully settle in their allotments (see Numbers 32:1–42; Joshua 1:12–15). The eastern tribes did their duty. And now the conquest is over and the eastern tribes begin to occupy and settle their land.

The author first provides the general area of settlement of the eastern tribes. The boundaries are as follows: to the south, the Arnon River valley; to the west, the Jordan River; to the north, Mount Hermon; and to the east, the eastern desert lands. The

Israelites captured most of this region, but the tribes did not dispossess all the inhabitants of the region; they 'did not drive out the Geshurites or the Maacathites' (13:13). Geshur is a small kingdom to the north-east of the Sea of Galilee, and Maacah lies still further north of it. The country of Geshur continues to have influence even into the time of David in the tenth century BC (see 2 Samuel 13:37-38; 14:23,32).

The author wants the reader to be clear that the tribe of Levi did *not* receive any inheritance on the east side of the Jordan River (13:14). It is mentioned here that 'the offerings by fire' that the Israelites give to the Lord are part of the inheritance of the Levites (cf. Numbers 18:21-24).

The Reubenite inheritance (13:15-23)

The biblical writer now presents a detailed picture of the tribal inheritance of the Reubenites in particular. The border of their allotment on the south is the Arnon River valley (13:16); to the west it is the Jordan River and the Dead Sea (13:23); to the north the boundary is the city of Heshbon (13:17,26); and to the east it is the desert regions. Sihon, king of the Amorites, controlled all of this land before Israel defeated him and took possession of his land (Numbers 21:24-26).

The writer adds one historical note with regard to the capture and settlement of the Reubenites. It says that the Israelite army killed many people in this region, including Balaam the son of Beor. Balaam was the central figure of an episode narrated in Numbers 22-24, in which the king of Moab summoned him to pronounce a curse on the people of Israel. Instead of cursing Israel, however, Balaam proclaimed a series of blessings on the covenant nation. At the close of the episode the text says that 'Balaam rose and went back to his place' (Numbers 24:25). That is not the last time we read of Balaam in a historical context: according to Numbers 31:16, Balaam gave Israel some counsel that 'caused the people of Israel to act treacherously against the LORD in the incident of Peor' (this refers to the Baal Peor incident in Numbers 25:1–5). Because Balaam led Israel astray they 'killed Balaam the son of Beor with the sword' (Numbers 31:8).

Balaam is also 'known from an extra-biblical text found at the site of Tell Deir 'Alla, a site located near the point where the Jabbok River enters the Jordan Valley. The Deir 'Alla inscription begins, "Warnings from the book of Balaam son of Beor. He was a seer of the gods." The inscription dates to around 800 BC, although it reflects an origin of a much earlier date.'[1]

The Gadite inheritance (13:24–28)
The tribal territory allotted to Gad by Moses is now described in detail. Its southern border is the northern boundary of the Reubenite territory near Heshbon (13:26); to the west Gad's tribal inheritance includes the entire Jordan River valley from the Dead Sea north to the Sea of Galilee, and that valley serves as its western border; to the north the Jabbok River is the border except for a sliver of land that extends to the city of Ramoth-gilead; and to the east it is the city of Aroer on the edge of the desert (13:25). Much of this land had belonged to the northern regions of the kingdom of Sihon, king of the Amorites, who ruled from Heshbon (13:27).

The inheritance of the half tribe of Manasseh (13:29–31)
The borders of the territory allotted to the half-tribe of Manasseh are as follows: the Jabbok River along the southern border of Bashan (13:30); the Jordan River valley to the west (north and south of the Sea of Galilee); to the north, Mount

Hermon; and the desert regions to the east. These lands, prior to the Israelite conquest, belonged to 'the kingdom of Og king of Bashan' (13:30).

Summary (13:32–33)

Verse 32 is a summary statement concerning the territories allotted by Moses to the two and a half tribes on the eastern side of the Jordan River. Seven times in chapter 13 the author declares that Moses is the one who granted this land to the tribes: this is emphatic to show that it was by the authority of this covenant mediator, this servant of God, that these tribes received their inheritance. The legitimacy of their allotment ought never to be called into question!

Another point of emphasis is found in verse 33. The Levites do not receive any land inheritance on the east side of the Jordan River. This fact was already stated in verse 14 of the chapter. But there is a difference between the two statements. Verse 14 states that the Levites were not granted land because their inheritance is 'the offerings by fire to the Lord'. The present verse gives another reason: 'The Lord God of Israel is their inheritance.' These two are not in opposition, but verse 33 is more comprehensive, deeper, richer and encompasses verse 14. The reality is that the tithes and offerings of Israel belong to the Lord, and he gives them to the Levites as part of their inheritance.

Points to ponder

1. Believers have an inheritance awaiting them in heaven

Israel's inheritance of the land of Canaan has a typological significance for the church. It is a pointer to the possession that believers will receive in the heavenly kingdom. The apostle Peter states, 'According to his great mercy, he has caused us to be born again to a living hope through the resurrection of Jesus Christ from the dead, to an inheritance that is imperishable, undefiled, and unfading, kept in heaven for you' (1 Peter 1:3–4). The Greek word Peter uses for 'inheritance' is the same word the Greek Old Testament (the Septuagint) uses when speaking of Israel's inheritance in the land of promise. Christians, therefore, are on a path that has an end in sight (a *telos*). We are heading for the celestial city, the city with foundations, and the land that will never perish or fade away—our inheritance! One of the Puritan prayers in *The Valley of Vision* puts it well:

> May I feel that I am a stranger and a pilgrim on earth,
> Declaring plainly that I seek a country,
> My title to it becoming daily more clear,
> My meetness [i.e. fitness] for it more perfect,
> My foretastes of it more abundant;
> And whatsoever I do, may it be done in the Saviour's name.[2]

2. The impact of this hope on the Christian's daily life

The truth that the believer's land inheritance awaits in heaven ought to have a deep impact on how the Christian walks out his pilgrimage through the earth. Richard Baxter, the great Puritan author, who wrote such works as *The Reformed Pastor* and *The Saint's Everlasting Rest*, was a frail invalid for most of his life. What kept him going in life and in his performance of spectacular duties for Christ? His secret was simple: each day he spent half an hour meditating on the life to come, thus putting at the forefront of his day the glory that awaited him. J. I. Packer comments on Baxter's practice: 'Diligent cultivation of hope gave him daily doggedness in disciplined hard work for God, despite the debilitating effect each day of his sick body.' One of the reasons Baxter was a good worker in the vineyard for Christ despite his sickness was that he looked to the celestial city; his eyes were upon the heavenly city, the city with foundations.

D. L. Moody put it this way: 'Take courage. We walk in the wilderness today and in the Promised Land tomorrow.'

18

Introduction to the distribution of the land west of the Jordan

Please read Joshua 14:1–15

Chapters 14–19 of the book of Joshua describe the distribution of the land of Canaan to the nine and a half tribes. The details of the allotments are bounded on both ends by individual land grants imparted to Caleb and Joshua (14:13; 19:49–50). These two grants serve as an *inclusio*, or outer frame, of the entire allocation of the land west of the Jordan. Joshua and Caleb were the two spies who 'wholly followed the Lord' (14:8,9,14) in the wilderness (Numbers 13–14). Whereas all the rest of their generation died in the wilderness because of unfaithfulness, Joshua and Caleb were spared and rewarded for their obedience to the Lord. Their reward is a land inheritance in Canaan. The point of the *inclusio* is to serve as a demonstration to all Israel: if they are obedient to the Lord, then they will also take possession of, and enjoy, their inheritance in the land!

The pivotal passage in the narrative of the land distribution is Joshua 18:1-10, in which the entire assembly of Israel gathers at Shiloh in front of the Tent of Meeting. Preceding that incident Joshua presents land grants to the tribes of Judah, Ephraim and the half-tribe of Manasseh from his headquarters in Gilgal (15:1–17:18). After the assembly at the Tent of Meeting at Shiloh, Joshua apportions the remainder of the land by lots to the remaining tribes (18:11–19:48).

Allocation of land west of the Jordan (14:1-5)

In the opening verse of this chapter the author provides the administrative structure which is to oversee the allocation of the land to the tribes on the west side of the Jordan River. Moses established this governance in Numbers 34:16-29. At the head of the list of overseers is Eleazar, who had succeeded Aaron as high priest of Israel (Numbers 20:22-29; Deuteronomy 10:6); he represents the priesthood of Israel in this activity. Next in line is Joshua, the son of Nun, who replaced Moses as covenant mediator (Deuteronomy 31:1-8). These two men preside over the entire affair and, then, acting under their authority are ten leaders, one from each of the nine and a half tribes.

The location of each tribal inheritance is determined by lot (14:2; cf. Numbers 33:54-56). 'The casting of lots was a common ancient Near-Eastern practice. This is one of the means by which God revealed his will and providence to his people in the Old Testament.'[1] Distribution of land by lot guarantees that it is by divine appointment, and that fact should help to prevent any type of land-grabbing or jockeying for position among the tribes. Divine apportionment would also help to protect Israel's leaders from showing favouritism to any one tribe. Allotment of the land is ultimately God's work.

The Levites do not receive any land inheritance during this allocation; nor did they inherit any territory when the eastern lands were given (13:14,33). However, verse 4 anticipates the cities and pasturelands that the Levites will acquire among all the tribes and that are granted in Joshua 21.

Caleb's land claim (14:6–9)

At this time Joshua resides in Gilgal. This was the first place of Israelite encampment after the people had crossed the Jordan River from the east (4:19). Gilgal has served as Joshua's headquarters since that time (see 5:10; 9:6; 10:6,15,43). The tribe of Judah, probably through representatives, seeks an audience with Joshua at Gilgal. They come on behalf of one of their own: Caleb, son of Jephunneh, the Kenizzite (Numbers 13:6). Once access is granted, Caleb speaks directly to Joshua.

He begins by saying, literally, 'You, you know ...' The addition in the text of the independent personal pronoun ('you') is emphatic, and, indeed, Joshua knows all that Caleb is about to say because he himself was a central character in that story. Caleb further adds that the matter is 'concerning you and me' (14:6). He reminds Joshua that the Lord spoke to Moses about Caleb and Joshua in Kadesh-barnea; this communication took place forty-five years prior to this meeting in Gilgal (Numbers 14:24; Deuteronomy 1:36–38).

The basis of the Lord's speaking to Moses about Caleb and Joshua was the event when the Israelite spies were sent on reconnaissance in the land of Canaan (Numbers 13:1–24). Moses, by command of God, sent twelve spies, one from each tribe, to scout the land—two of the spies were Caleb and Joshua. When the scouting party returned to Kadesh-barnea, Caleb gave a minority report: he argued that Israel would be able to capture the land. The other scouts forcefully disputed his claim, and they 'made the heart of the people melt' (14:8). On the basis of this majority report, the people broke into an open rebellion (Numbers 14:1–12).

One of God's responses to the incident was to reward Caleb 'because he ... has followed me fully' (Numbers 14:24; the same verb that is used here in 14:8). The Lord promised that Caleb and his posterity would inherit some land in Canaan (Numbers 14:24; Deuteronomy 1:36). And, now, forty-five years later, Caleb comes before Joshua to collect on that promise.

Caleb requests an inheritance in the highlands (14:10-12)

One of the reasons that the majority of spies did not want to invade the land of Canaan was the presence of the sons of Anak (Numbers 13:33). These large people, who are compared to the giant Nephilim mentioned in Genesis 6:4, instilled great fear in the scouts. At the time of Caleb's meeting with Joshua at Gilgal some of the Anakim still reside in the Judaean hill country (see Numbers 13:22). Caleb, ever the warrior, wants his inheritance to be in the area where the feared Anakim still dwell (14:12). Caleb is hopeful that he will be able to drive out the Anakim from his land possession.

And why not? Although Caleb is 'this day eighty-five years old', he is as vigorous and hardy as in the day Moses sent the spies into the land of Canaan from Kadesh-barnea. That was forty-five years ago. Caleb announces that he is just as strong for battle and 'for going and coming'. The latter phrase is a formula used in the Old Testament to reflect a person's ability to lead, in particular for military leadership (see Numbers 27:17; Deuteronomy 31:2; 1 Kings 3:7). Caleb is saying that, even at his advanced age, he has retained those leadership qualities. Most people have certainly lost many of their physical and mental faculties by this age; not so Caleb! And, in fact, he is so fit that he is looking for a fight!

Hebron (14:13–15)

Joshua responds to Caleb's request by assigning the city of Hebron as his inheritance. Hebron is located on the highest peak of the Judaean highlands. It was from here that Abraham and Lot divided the land (Genesis 13:8–11), and it was here that the patriarchs Abraham, Isaac and Jacob were buried. Under Joshua's leadership, the Israelite forces conquered Hebron during the southern campaign (10:29–39). He also rid the hill country of the Anakim so that 'there was none of the Anakim left in the land' (11:22). However, it appears that Hebron has fallen back into the hands of the Anakim after the conquest. Caleb will have to fight them to claim his rightful inheritance (see 15:13–19).

After Caleb secures his inheritance, then 'the land had rest from war'. This announcement echoes Joshua 11:23, which says, 'Joshua took the whole land ... and ... gave it for an inheritance to Israel ... And the land had rest from war.' This does not mean that there are no skirmishes between the tribes of Israel and the Canaanites (see, e.g., Judges 1), but, in general, major warfare and conquest are over.

Points to ponder

1. Caleb is a great example of one who was valiant in the faith

He 'wholly followed the LORD' despite what the world told him, or even what the other Israelite spies said to him! What J. C. Ryle said about Noah (apart from the specific references to building the ark) could easily have been penned about Caleb:

> How was it that Noah persevered in building the ark? He stood alone amidst a world of sinners and unbelievers. He had to endure scorn, ridicule and mockery. What was it that nerved his arm, and made him patiently work on and face it all? It was faith. He believed in a wrath to come. He believed that there was no safety, excepting in the ark that he was preparing. Believing, he held the world's opinion very cheap. He counted the cost by faith, and had no doubt that to build the ark was gain.

All Christians are to stand tall and be courageous, even when the odds are against them. The Earl of Dartmouth (1731–1811) was a strong Christian and a soldier of the gospel. He knew some of the great preachers of his day through his acquaintance with Lady Huntingdon: he met Whitefield, Romaine and the Wesleys. His faith was well known; a letter from a Mr Hervey to Lady Shirley in 1757 speaks of it: 'I have not the honour of Lord Dartmouth's acquaintance; but I hear he is full of grace, and valiant for the truth—a lover of Christ, and an ornament to the gospel.' Lord Dartmouth was the butt of jokes and ridicule at the hands of the upper crust of society. Many of them, however, were eventually won over to Christ by Dartmouth's stand for the Lord. King George III knew of Dartmouth's faith; in an interview with Dr Beattie, the king said, 'They call my Lord Dartmouth an enthusiast, but surely he says nothing on the subject of religion but what any Christian may and ought to say.'

2. Caleb was also a great example to the Israelites of his day

The Lord commanded Israel to clean out the land by expelling its pagan inhabitants (Numbers 32:21; 33:52). Caleb is itching to get on with it in his land inheritance. He is looking to pick a fight with the Anakim so that he might 'drive them out just as the LORD said' (14:12). Caleb, although eighty-five years old, is like a dog straining at the leash! All the Israelites should have had this zeal and fervour as they attempted to secure and populate their land inheritance, but that did not turn out to be the case.

Oh that we had such enthusiasm for the gospel, for obedience to God's Word and for evangelism. William Guthrie, pastor of a church in Fenwick, Scotland, during the seventeenth century, had such a zeal for the salvation of souls. On one occasion he was travelling home from a meeting when he got lost in the darkness and mist of the moor. He prayed that God would lead him to safety. Eventually he made it to a farmer's house and he was given safe haven for that evening. The lady of the house was in the throes of death, and a Catholic priest was there giving her the last rites. After the priest left, Guthrie went to the woman and asked if she had received peace to die. She said she had not. So Guthrie shared the gospel with her, and he prayed that her heart would be opened to the truth. His prayer was answered as she died rejoicing in the Saviour. When he finally made it home, his worried wife asked where he had spent the night. He said, 'I came to a farmhouse where I saw a great wonder. I found a woman in a state of nature; I saw her in a state of grace; and I left her in a state of glory.'

Oh that we had such enthusiasm for our eternal inheritance! In John Bunyan's allegory *Pilgrim's Progress* there is a telling conversation between a man named Obstinate and a man named Christian that reflects the type of fervour a believer ought to have for the celestial city:

Obstinate: 'What are the things you seek, since you leave all the world to find them?'

Christian: 'I seek an inheritance, incorruptible, undefiled, and that fadeth not away; and it is laid up in Heaven, and fast there, to be bestowed at the time appointed, on them that diligently seek it. Read it so, if you will, in my book.'

19

Judah's allotment

Please read Joshua 15:1–63

Some ladies in my church decided as a group to read through the Bible in a year. Of course, I greatly encouraged them in this endeavour. Soon, however, they came to me complaining that they had hit a brick wall; they had arrived at the genealogy of Genesis 5, and they had no idea how to deal with it. Why is it there? What is its purpose? And, indeed, reading all those names that can barely be pronounced is tedious and boring! I believe we get the same reaction from people today who read the land allotments of Joshua 15–19. As Ralph Davis comments, these don't 'exactly stir sermonic juices or suggest warm devotional thoughts'.[1] Why are they there, and why does the author go on and on with boundary lists and names of cities?

The first point that we need to consider is that 'All Scripture is breathed out by God and profitable for teaching, for reproof, for correction, and for training in righteousness, that the man

of God may be competent, equipped for every good work'
(2 Timothy 3:16–17). And so, as believers, we must come to
the land-grant texts with the conviction that they have been
provided and preserved by the Holy Spirit for our benefit and
edification. We are thus required to work hard to interpret these
texts properly and to apply them appropriately to the church
and to the individual Christian.

In this regard we should not overlook the significance of the
land grants to the people of God at the time they were made.
The promise of God to Abraham that his descendants would
inherit and occupy the land of Canaan was given almost 500
years before the land distribution under Joshua (Genesis 12:7).
For much of that time the people had been in slavery in Egypt
and wandering in the wilderness. Now, here and finally, the land
of promise is conferred upon them. The great promise of God
is coming to pass, and therefore the allocation of the land is
related in great detail. In chapter 15 the biblical author adoringly
traces the boundaries of the land assigned to the tribe of Judah
and affectionately lists many of the towns within its borders.

What a precious text this would have been to the tribe of
Judah! This reminds me of a house that my wife and I recently
purchased. With the house came multiple documents, or 'spec.
sheets'; these include page after page of the house specifications,
such as the size of the water heater, the grade of insulation, the
type of shingles used for the roof, and hundreds of other details
relating to the construction of the building. I read every single
page with great interest and I gave attention to every detail.
Someone else could look at these documents and say, 'These are
boring and tedious! What do they have to do with me?' So, as we
consider the inheritance of Judah we should remember that the

original audience of that tribe would have relished every detail of the description of their land allotment!

It is also important for us to observe that the tribe of Judah receives the first allocation of land among the tribes of Israel. Judah, however, was the fourth son of Jacob born to Leah (Genesis 29:32–35). Why then does this tribe receive the first inheritance? In Genesis 49, Jacob blessed his sons (and the tribes that would descend from them). Judah received a special blessing: he would rule over his brothers, and the great king of Israel would come from him (Genesis 49:8–12). What we are witnessing in the order of the land distribution in Canaan is the ascendancy of the tribe of Judah to a position of leadership in the tribal confederation of Israel.

The boundaries of the tribal allotment of Judah (15:1–12)
Not only does the tribe of Judah receive the first allotment of land, it also acquires the largest distribution of territory. Its land grant lies in the southernmost regions of Canaan. The southern border extends from the south end of the Dead Sea westward just south of Kadesh-barnea, and then along the Brook of Egypt (= Wadi el-Arish) to the Mediterranean Sea (15:1–4). The western boundary of the allotment is the Mediterranean Sea (15:12). Its eastern border is the entire Dead Sea and the land of Edom (15:5). The northern border extends westward from the north tip of the Dead Sea at the Jordan River to Jerusalem and then to Beth Shemesh and, finally, to the Mediterranean Sea.

One important point that needs to be understood is that the tribal allotments do not necessarily reflect the land that each tribe actually inhabits after the conquest. The reality is that several tribes, including Judah, have to continue the process of defeating and driving out the Canaanites from their inheritance—some tribes are more successful in this than others (19:40–48). In addition, it is also clear that some tribes end up controlling portions of territory that had been allotted to other tribes (see 17:11–13).

The wars of Caleb (15:13–19)

These verses are a historical insertion in the text to demonstrate that Caleb acts upon the inheritance that had been given to him in Joshua 14:13–15. Caleb dispossesses the three sons of Anak from the city of Hebron (15:13–14). 'Sheshai', 'Ahiman' and 'Talmai' are probably either family or clan designations, so that Caleb defeated more than merely three men, but rather three people groups. These 'descendants of Anak' were the ones who had inspired fear in the Israelite scouts in Numbers 13–14. Now Caleb drives them out of the Hebron area. In this episode, Caleb is a paradigm, or example, for how the Israelite tribes are to act; they are to be aggressive and forceful in their removal of the Canaanites from the land of promise.

Apparently Caleb is not satisfied with cleaning out the area of Hebron, but, as a member of the tribe of Judah, he wants to help dispossess the Canaanites of a larger region that belongs to Judah. He thus makes a raid against the city of Debir, which is located eight miles to the south-west of Hebron at the modern site of Khirbet Rabud (15:15). The Israelites originally captured this site during the conquest (10:38–39), but obviously it has fallen back into the hands of the Canaanites.

In verse 16, Caleb offers his daughter as the prize for whoever captures Debir. Calvin says about this offer:

> And it appears, that when he held out this rare prize to his fellow-soldiers for taking the city, no small achievement

was required. This confirms what formerly seemed to be the case, that it was a dangerous and difficult task which had been assigned him, when he obtained his conditional grant. Accordingly, with the view of urging the bravest to exert themselves, he promises his daughter in marriage as a reward to the valour of the man who should first scale the wall.[2]

Such an offer may signify that this job was viewed by Caleb as an insurmountable task.

No matter how great the difficulty, Othniel, the son of Kenaz, captures the city of Debir (15:17). This is the same man who later serves as one of the judges of Israel, delivers the people from the oppression of Cushan-rishathaim and gives the land of Israel peace for forty years (Judges 3:7–11). Thus he is a mighty and courageous warrior. He also comes from good fighting stock: he is Caleb's nephew (Judges 3:9).

Caleb gives his daughter Achsah to Othniel. It appears that her dowry may have been 'the land of the Negeb' (15:19). The term 'Negeb' literally means 'south country', and so Caleb deeds to her a parcel of land to the south of Hebron. The precise location of her marriage gift is uncertain: the region of the Negeb is large, extending from the hills south of Hebron to the site of Kadesh-barnea in the south. The Negeb is famous for scarcity of water, and so, Achsah comes to Caleb to ask for 'springs of water'. Caleb obliges her by presenting her with both the upper and the lower springs. Where these springs are located is unknown.

Cities of Judah's inheritance (15:20–63)

In addition to the borders of Judah's inheritance, the biblical author now enumerates the various cities within Judah's allotment. These towns, 'with their villages', are listed according to four regions of the inheritance: the south (15:21–32); the Shephelah, or lowlands (15:33–47); the highlands (15:48–60); and the 'wilderness', or desert areas (15:61–62). Well over one hundred cities are recorded in these verses. Why would the biblical author go into such detail by listing city after city in Judah's estate? This catalogue of cities simply gives 'concrete expression to the fulfilment of God's promises regarding the land'.[3] In other words, it demonstrates that the accomplishment of God's word to Israel has indeed taken place in space and time; it is a historical fact that is tangible and concrete. There is a true earthiness to this inheritance.

At the time of the writing of the book of Joshua ('to this day') the tribe of Judah has not been able to dispossess the Jebusites who inhabit the city of Jerusalem; thus the list ends on an ominous note (15:63). Although Caleb has been quite successful in ridding his inheritance of Canaanites, the tribe of Judah makes much less progress overall. In fact, it is not until the time of David that Israel captures the city of Jerusalem (2 Samuel 5:7).[4]

Points to ponder

1. The solid reality of our inheritance as Christians

As the tribe of Judah is reminded in this chapter of the earthly reality of their inheritance, Christians, the new Israel, ought to keep in view that our inheritance as well is solid, substantial and corporeal. The common 'pie-in-the-sky' view of heavenly existence, in which believers float about on clouds while carrying harps, is not mere distortion, but it is unbiblical. As A. Hoekema comments, 'One gets the impression from certain hymns that glorified believers will spend eternity in some ethereal heaven somewhere off in space.'[5] In reality, our allotment of a new heaven and a new earth is not some dirtless, fleshless entity. But it is real, substantive and actual land.

2. The abundance of our inheritance

When we read the details of Judah's inheritance—how large it is and how many cities it includes—the reader is not only to be struck by the concreteness of the inheritance, but also by the abundance of it. We too, as Christians, ought to be in awe and relish the rich and full nature of our heavenly inheritance. Horatius Bonar expresses it well when he says:

> The hope of the Christian is a hope full of immortality; a hope which God himself gives, and of which no man can rob us. It is divine and everlasting. It brings with it the peace which passes all understanding; and it contains in it a joy unspeakable and full of glory. There is no disappointment in it ... It is sure and glorious, like Jesus Christ, from whom it comes. It is connected with a crown, with an inheritance, with a kingdom, with a glory that does not fade away, and with an eternity of joy.

May we live each day in the light of this certain and rich inheritance—a hope as sure as the Saviour on whom it rests!

20

Allotment for the tribes of Joseph

Please read Joshua 16:1–17:18

I n the last chapter Judah received the first distribution of
land in Canaan. His pre-eminence is right because Jacob had
blessed him above all the other tribes: he would rule over
his brothers and the great king would come from him (Genesis
49:8–12). The second allotment, and the final one made from
the camp at Gilgal, is granted to the tribes of Ephraim and the
half-tribe of Manasseh. In Genesis 49, Jacob had also given these
tribes a wonderful blessing and a privileged position among
the tribes of Israel (vv. 22–26). After these allotments at Gilgal
one perhaps sees the beginnings of a rivalry between Judah
and Ephraim even at this early stage of settlement. Almost
immediately Joshua warns these two tribes to stay clear of one
another and not to cross borders against one another (18:5).

The struggle and animosity between Judah and Ephraim will
have far-reaching implications and consequences. At this point

I want to quote at length a summary of this issue that I have published elsewhere:

> A first attempt to establish a monarchy in Israel was made by the tribe of Ephraim (Judges 8:22ff.), and a second attempt was also made by them (Judges 9:7–16,22). And indeed, the position of Ephraim in the tribal hierarchy was strengthened because of the presence of the tabernacle in its tribal allotment: at Shechem, Bethel, and Shiloh. That, of course, would later cause problems when the temple was built in Jerusalem, on the northern border of the tribe of Judah. It also became an issue of conflict when the kingship in Israel was not established under an Ephraimite king. In regard to God's choice of a king, the psalmist declared, 'He rejected the tent of Joseph; he did not choose the tribe of Ephraim, but he chose the tribe of Judah, Mount Zion, which he loves... He chose David his servant ... to shepherd Jacob his people, Israel his inheritance" (Psalm 78:67–68,70a,71b). The evidence of a division and rivalry was clear during the kingship of Saul (see 1 Samuel 11:8; 18:16). David ruled first over Judah for seven and a half years, and then over all Israel, including Judah, for 33 years (2 Samuel 2:4; 5:5)... The roots of the division that would occur after the death of Solomon, therefore, were long-standing and deep-seated. Solomon added to the conflict by making the burdens of taxation less on Judah than on the other tribes (1 Kings 4). Jeroboam, an Ephraimite (1 Kings 11:26), thus led a revolt against the monarchy in Jerusalem, and all Israel followed him, and they cried out ... 'What portion do we have in David? We have no inheritance in the son of Jesse. To your tents, O Israel! Look now to your own house, David' (1 Kings 12:16; cf. 2 Samuel 20:1).[1]

The southern border of the tribes of Joseph (16:1–4)

The text begins with the phrase, translated literally, 'The lot came out for the sons of Joseph ...' This perhaps indicates that, in the process of casting lots, some type of vessel is used, out of which the lots came when it was tossed. One lot is cast for the two tribes, the half-tribe of Manasseh and that of Ephraim—in other words, the sons of Joseph.

These introductory verses only describe the southern boundary of the tribal inheritance of the sons of Joseph. This border begins at the Jordan River just north of the city of Jericho and it extends westward across the highlands to the town of Bethel. From there it crosses into the Shephelah at Gezer and continues into the coastal plain, where it ends at the Mediterranean Sea. The allotment does not include the city of Jericho because the latter is part of the inheritance of Benjamin (18:21). The other borders of the sons of Joseph are set out in the descriptions in subsequent verses of the inheritance of the individual holdings of the half-tribe of Manasseh and of Ephraim.

Ephraim's allotment (16:5–9)

The genealogical descent of the sons of Joseph is given in the proper order in verse 4: 'Manasseh and Ephraim'. However, in the distribution of the land, the tribe of the younger son Ephraim receives priority over the tribe of the elder son Manasseh. The pre-eminence and privilege of the tribe of Ephraim reflect the episode in Genesis when Jacob elevates Ephraim over Manasseh in the blessings given to the sons of Joseph (Genesis 48:13–20). Verse 20 of that passage declares, 'Thus he put Ephraim before Manasseh.'

Identification of the precise borders of Ephraim's inheritance is fraught with difficulties. We simply do not know the location of a number of the sites mentioned in the textual description. However, there are enough geographical locators that we do know for a general sketch of the extent of the territory to be drawn. The southern border of Ephraim has already been given in verses 1–3, and it appears here in abbreviated form (16:5–6). The northern boundary is pin-pointed at the site of Michmethath, which lies near the town of Shechem in the central highlands (16:6). From Michmethath the border runs south-east to Jericho, where it meets the southern boundary of the allotment. The western boundary is 'at the sea' (16:8), namely the Mediterranean.

A city list, like the one given for Judah (15:21–63), is not provided for Ephraim. The only towns mentioned are the ones that belong to Ephraim although they are located 'within the inheritance of the Manassites' (16:9). Why Ephraim has possession of some towns in Manasseh is unclear, although it may in some way reflect the pre-eminent status of the tribe of Ephraim over that of Manasseh.

Manasseh's allotment (17:1–6)

The opening two verses in this chapter define the clans of Manasseh that receive allotments of land. First, the biblical writer states that the Manassites had already received the lands of Gilead and Bashan in Transjordan. These territories had been deeded by Moses to the clan of Machir prior to the conquest of Canaan. This is the inheritance of the half-tribe of Manasseh on the other side of the Jordan River. Now the other half of the tribe of Manasseh is receiving its land distribution in Canaan according to its clans: Abiezer, Helek, Asriel, Shechem, Hepher and Shemida.

There is one problem with the Manassite inheritance. In the book of Numbers, the five daughters of Zelophehad, the son of Hepher (one of the clans mentioned above), approached Moses about an issue: Zelophehad has no sons, only daughters (Numbers 27:1–11). 'The ancient Israelite custom was that inheritance descended through the sons and, in particular, the law is very firm concerning the rights of the firstborn son (Deuteronomy 21:15–17).'[2] The daughters of Zelophehad presented their case to Moses that they should receive a land possession in the name of their father. Moses took the request to the Lord, who agreed to the daughters' request. In the present passage, the daughters approach the leaders of Israel to stake their claim, and they 'received an inheritance along with his sons' (17:6). Thus, there are ten portions to Manasseh's inheritance in Canaan: five to the sons of Manasseh (excluding Hepher) and five to the daughters of Zelophehad.

The borders of the half-tribe of Manasseh (17:7–13)

In these verses the author presents the boundaries of the territory inherited by the half-tribe of Manasseh in Canaan. The northern border is the tribe of Asher in the west (17:7) and the tribe of Issachar in the east (17:10). The boundary to the west is the Mediterranean Sea (17:9), and to the east is the Jordan River. The southern border sits at Michmethath (17:7) and the northern border of the inheritance of Ephraim.

Details of the cities that form part of Manasseh's inheritance are not provided as they are for Judah's territory (15:21–63). Some cities are listed that belong to Manasseh, although they are located within the territories of the tribes of Asher and Issachar: Beth-shean, Ibleam, Dor, En-dor, Taanach and Megiddo. All of these cities, except Dor, lay within the Esdraelon Plain. Although these cities are deeded to the Manassites, the tribe does not control or occupy them. The Canaanites 'persisted' and were determined to remain sovereign over these cities (17:12).

Although the Israelites grow stronger, and they put the Canaanites to forced labour, they are still unable to drive them from the land completely (17:13). The incomplete nature of the Israelite occupation echoes throughout the land-distribution texts (15:63; 16:10; 19:47).

The complaint of the sons of Joseph (17:14–18)

The sons of Joseph respond to the news of their allotment with dissatisfaction. In verse 14, they take issue with the lot that has fallen to them, and with the fact that they have received only one lot. They are arguing that they have too many people to be limited to the territory given to them. In addition, the tribes complain that the Lord has blessed them 'all along', or, literally, 'up to this point', but this mere single allotment is not a continuation of God's blessings to them. This verse thus reflects severe discontent on the part of these one and a half tribes. In reality, their reasoning is disingenuous and specious.

In the first place, according to the census of Numbers 26, the number of people in each of these tribes is not all that great and is, in fact, less than that of some of the other tribes. Manasseh has a military enrolment of 52,700 men and Ephraim has one of 32,500 men (Numbers 26:28–37). In comparison, Issachar has 64,300 men of military age; Zebulun has 60,500; Dan has 64,400; and Judah is the largest with 76,500 (Numbers 26:19–27,42–43). It thus appears that Ephraim and Manasseh are making an exaggerated claim.

In addition, their charge that they have only one lot for an inheritance is untrue, since half of the tribe of Manasseh has already received a large territorial tract in Transjordan.

This discontent of the one and a half tribes also flies directly in the face of the providence of God. Allotment is by divine apportionment through the casting of lots (14:1–2). To put it simply, it is God's will that these tribes receive this allotment, but they complain about it.

Part of the problem is that much of the inheritance is forested and not conducive to ease of settlement. Joshua's answer is that the one and a half tribes need to penetrate the wooded areas, clear the ground and make the land more easily cultivable and liveable. The archaeological record shows that at this time many new settlements appear in areas of the highlands that had never before been settled. To support this human settlement, new or borrowed methods of agriculture are used by the Israelites. One such development is the use of agricultural terracing, which transforms hilly slopes into flat areas for cultivation.

The one and a half tribes apparently do not like Joshua's answer: they flatly pronounce that the hill country is not 'enough', or 'sufficient', for them (17:16). Yet, they show fear of expansion into the valley areas because of the presence of the Canaanites who have chariots of iron. This fear is not to be complimented or lauded. It contrasts strongly with Caleb's fearlessness and his aggressiveness to fight the Canaanites and to drive them from the land (14:6–15). The fearlessness they should have reminds me of Churchill's great speech to Britain in June 1940:

We shall go on to the end,

we shall fight in France,

we shall fight on the seas and oceans,

we shall fight with growing confidence and growing strength in the air,

we shall defend our Island, whatever the cost may be,

we shall fight on the beaches,

we shall fight on the landing grounds,

we shall fight in the fields and in the streets,

we shall fight in the hills;

we shall never surrender, and even if, which I do not for a moment believe, this Island or a large part of it were subjugated and starving, then our Empire beyond the seas, armed and guarded by the British Fleet, would carry on the struggle, until, in God's good time, the New World, with all its power and might, steps forth to the rescue and the liberation of the old.

Like Caleb, Israel as a whole needs to be willing to confront the Canaanites, no matter where they are in the land.

Joshua repeats his charge to these tribes (17:17–18). There is enough land for them if they will only clear the land of forests and drive out the Canaanites from their inheritance. The tribes do not want to do these things. The timidity of the Ephraimites, in particular, becomes proverbial in later Israelite history (see

Psalm 78:9-10). Joshua is quite aware of their hesitation, and so in verse 18 alone he uses the Hebrew word *ki* five times. The best translation of this word in the context is as the emphatic particle 'indeed'. I would therefore suggest the following reading: '*Indeed* the hill country shall be yours; *indeed* it is a forest, but you shall clear it and it shall be yours to its extremities; *indeed* you will drive out the Canaanites: *indeed* they have chariots of iron; *indeed* they are strong.' Indeed!

Points to ponder

1. A warning against discontent

The discontent of Ephraim and the half-tribe of Manasseh with the lot that God had granted to them reminds me of how often Christians complain about their lot in life. There is nothing new under the sun. In 1 Corinthians 10:9-11, the apostle Paul warns us by making mention of the murmurings of the Israelites in the wilderness:

> We must not put Christ to the test, as some of them did and were destroyed by serpents, nor grumble, as some of them did and were destroyed by the Destroyer. Now these things happened to them as an example, but they were written down for our instruction, on whom the end of the ages has come.

We are not to complain about the providence of God even in the direst circumstances. The Puritan Gerrard Winstanley, in the midst of severe persecution, said, 'Whatsoever your condition is, murmur not at it, but wait.' We need to guard ourselves against anxious murmuring: during times of great oppression Edward Burrough said, 'Why should we murmur against God? Or say, why hast thou done it?'

All of us can understand the desire to grumble during hardship and affliction; it is not right, but it is easy to comprehend and to do. What we see with the Israelites is discontent in the midst of blessing and celebration. The land of promise is being distributed to the tribes of Israel! At last, the promises of God are coming to pass for the covenant people! Yet these tribes deny that they have been given enough—they want more! Oh, how like the Israelites we are! God's provision never seems sufficient for us. We always crave for more. Some would say, 'If I had a different job things would be better; if I didn't have to stay with the children all day things would be better; if I had more money ...; if I had a different spouse ...; if I had a better home ...' Let us not mock God by declaring that we are not satisfied with his provision for us.

2. Looking to the heavenly inheritance

This chapter is to remind the Christian one more time that there is an inheritance awaiting the people of God. True believers have always understood that there exists a heavenly inheritance; the author of the epistle to the Hebrews talks of the great men of faith in the Old Testament by declaring:

> These all died in faith, not having received the things promised, but having seen them and greeted them from afar, and having acknowledged that they were strangers and exiles on the earth. For people who speak thus make it clear that they are seeking a homeland. If they had been thinking of that land from which they had gone out, they would have had opportunity to return. But as it is, they desire a better country, that is, a heavenly one. Therefore God is not ashamed to be called their God, for he has prepared for them a city (Hebrews 11:13–16).

A celestial city, a heavenly inheritance! May we have eyes to see it through the mists of this life!

21

The remaining allotments

Please read Joshua 18:1–19:51

I have been preaching in my church through the book of Philippians for the last few months, but I am nearing the end of that study. So I announced last Sunday morning that when we finish Philippians we would begin a series on the prophet Haggai. One could have heard a pin drop. The silence, however, was not due to eagerness and excitement on the part of the congregation, but rather it was a glassy-eyed, yawn-filled response to one of the Minor Prophets. I could almost hear a chant go up: 'Boring! Boring!' The contemporary Christian listener or reader would obviously respond in a similar way to the two chapters in Joshua which we now turn to consider—a total lack of interest in the granting of one lot after another to seven of the tribes of Israel. What is the purpose of the geographical detail? Why are there lists and lists of cities and boundaries? How does this apply to me as a Christian?

A number of years ago I wrote a commentary on the book of Leviticus. In the preface I wrote the following:

> As I studied and commented on the book of Leviticus for the past few years, I often felt greatly weighed down. At times, the tedium often overwhelmed me. To be honest, the thought of giving up the commentary work was my partner as I went to my study each day. But as I daily persevered a new thought began to emerge, and now that I have finished the work the thought has become crystal clear. The laws of Leviticus are *meant* to weigh us down. As we read the laws, we are to realize our sinfulness (Romans 7:7), and our inability to keep the law. Leviticus highlights our guilt and condemnation before the Holy One of Israel.[1]

So, when we think about the detailed allotments before us in Joshua 18–19, there is one thing we can be sure of: the great attention and care taken by the biblical author in providing the details of the land distribution are purposeful and didactic. I would argue that the primary purpose of them is to give concrete expression and shape to the very promises of God to the patriarchs and others (Genesis 12:7; 13:15; 15:18, etc.). The promise of the land of Canaan to God's people is at the very core of the covenant between God and Israel. Thus, the major point of Joshua 18–19 is that God is a covenant-keeping and a promise-keeping God!

From Gilgal to Shiloh (18:1)

When Israel had first crossed the Jordan River into the land of Canaan, the people established their main encampment at Gilgal, which lies approximately two miles north-east of Jericho (4:19). Gilgal has remained the central camp for Israel and the headquarters for Joshua up to this point of the story; it is at

Gilgal that Joshua gave the first two allotments of land to Judah and to the sons of Joseph (14:6). But now the people assemble at the site of Shiloh, and there they erect the tabernacle, or 'tent of meeting'. Shiloh is located at modern Khirbet Seilun, and it lies in the very heart of the Ephraimite inheritance in the highlands.

Shiloh is the sacred religious centre of Israel from this time through the period of the book of Judges. The ark of the covenant resides in the tabernacle at Shiloh until the Philistines capture it in the battle of Ebenezer (1 Samuel 4). Eli serves as high priest at Shiloh (1 Samuel 1:3), and Samuel trains here for his ministry (1 Samuel 1:24). Shiloh also serves at this time as the new seat of Israelite political and military leadership: it is here that Joshua now allocates the remaining land to the tribes of Israel (18:1–19:51).

The act of dividing the remaining territory (18:2–7)

There are still seven tribes that have not received allotments in Canaan: they are, in alphabetical order, Asher, Benjamin, Dan, Issachar, Naphtali, Simeon and Zebulun. The tribes of Gad, Reuben and the half-tribe of Manasseh had already acquired their land in Transjordan by the command of Moses (18:7). Levi gets no allotment of land, 'for the priesthood of the LORD is their heritage' (18:7; cf. 13:14). And Joshua has already granted Judah and the sons of Joseph their inheritance in Canaan from Gilgal (15:1–17:18). These tribes are to 'continue', or, literally, 'stand', in their territories until the other tribes receive the apportionment of the remaining land (18:5). Thus, Judah, Ephraim and the half-tribe of Manasseh are not to make a land grab!

Joshua is critical of the tribes regarding their reserve and procrastination in taking possession of the land (18:3). The Hebrew verb translated here as 'put off' literally means 'to be slack'; the Israelites are simply being slow and negligent in their task (see 15:63; 16:10; 17:13). In response, Joshua commands that the seven tribes who have not yet received their inheritance supply three men from each tribe to scout and make a land survey of the remaining territory in Canaan, and then to bring the results back to him (18:4). At that point Joshua will cast lots before the Lord to determine the specific boundaries of each tribe's allotment (18:6).

Obedience of the seven tribes (18:8–10)

The seven tribes do exactly as Joshua has commanded. So twenty-one men traverse the land of Canaan, and they provide a survey of the territory still to be occupied. They then write the results, or description, of the survey 'in a book'; the Hebrew word for 'book' is a general one that can signify a scroll or some other material that may be written on. The surveyors return to Joshua with the book in hand, and, on the basis of the written results, the Israelite leader casts lots to distribute the land to the tribes (18:10).

We shall not spend a lot of time looking at the details of each tribal allotment; the geography and topography of the land assignments are readily available in other literature.[2] We shall, however, consider a few general matters regarding the locations of the tribal lots.

The inheritance of Benjamin (18:11–28)

The allotments of the seven tribes at Shiloh are granted according to the order, or rank, of the sons of Jacob. The sons of Jacob's two wives, Leah and Rachel, receive the first shares: Benjamin, Simeon, Zebulun and Issachar; later the sons of Jacob's concubines get their shares: Asher, Naphtali and Daniel

Benjamin was Jacob's second son by his favourite wife Rachel, and so he is placed at the head of the list.

Benjamin's inheritance lies between the territories of Judah to the south and the sons of Joseph to the north (18:11). Its northern boundary is the same as Ephraim's southern border (16:1–3) from the Jordan River at Jericho to the site of Beth-horon in the west. From Beth-horon the border abruptly turns south until it meets Judah's northern border at Kiriath-jearim: this is Benjamin's western border (18:14). Benjamin's southern border begins at Kiriath-jearim and goes east along Judah's northern border (15:5–9). The eastern border of Benjamin is the Jordan River (18:20).

As was the case with the tribe of Judah, the inheritance of Benjamin includes a city list: verses 21–24 itemize the towns in the eastern part of the allotment, and verses 25–28 those in the west. Some of these cities play a major role in the history of Israel: Jericho, Bethel, Gibeon, Jerusalem and Gibeah.

The inheritance of Simeon (19:1–9)

The tribe of Simeon does not receive an independent inheritance, but 'their inheritance was in the midst of the inheritance of the people of Judah' (19:1). This is in fulfilment of the indictment that Jacob brought against his two sons Simeon and Levi (Genesis 49:5–7). Because those two sons acted in blood vengeance on the Shechemites in response to the violation of Dinah (Genesis 34), Jacob said of them, 'I will divide them in Jacob and scatter them in Israel' (Genesis 49:7). Neither tribe receives an independent allotment of land in Canaan.

The boundaries of Simeon's inheritance are not provided in the text; they merely receive a series of cities that are near one another in the Negeb. The allotment consists of seventeen cities in the south-western sector of Judah's territory.

The inheritance of Zebulun (19:10–16)
The tribe of Zebulun receives the third lot given at Shiloh. Zebulun was the youngest son of Jacob's wife Leah (Genesis 30:20). His tribal descendants are granted their land inheritance prior to the tribe of Issachar, although Issachar was the older brother (Genesis 30:18). By right Issachar should appear first; however, Jacob had blessed Zebulun before his brother in Genesis 49:13–15 and Moses did the same in Deuteronomy 33:18. The reason for the switch is unknown, although it is perhaps comparable to what happened to Manasseh and Ephraim (Genesis 48:19–20).

Zebulun's land lies in Lower Galilee. It is land-locked, with Issachar on the south-east, Manasseh on the south-west, Asher on the north-west and Naphtali on the north-east.

The inheritance of Issachar (19:17–23)
Issachar's territory is primarily described with a list of cities. However, one boundary line is mentioned in the text, and it gives detail to the eastern part of the northern boundary that ends at the Jordan River (19:22). The bulk of the allotment consists of the lush and fertile Jezreel Valley. According to Jacob's blessing on Issachar in Genesis 49:14–15, the latter's main aim is to find a good resting-place and a land that is pleasant. Issachar's tribal inheritance reflects that blessing.

The inheritance of Asher (19:24–31)
In Genesis 49:20, Jacob said of his son Asher, 'Asher's food shall be rich, and he shall yield royal delicacies.' His 'prophecy for the tribe of Asher certainly comes true when the people

settle in Canaan ... Asher's allotment is in the western Galilee hill-country, an area famed for its lushness and fertility (Deuteronomy 33:24–25).[3] Asher's territory extends along the Mediterranean Sea from Mount Carmel in the south to Sidon in the north; to the east it is bordered by the Galilean hills and the inheritance of Naphtali.

The inheritance of Naphtali (19:32–39)
The tribe of Naphtali receives the sixth lot given at Shiloh. Its eastern border is the northern extension of the Jordan River that flows into the Sea of Galilee. The Litani River is probably its northern border. The territory of Asher is Naphtali's western border, and Zebulun's land forms the boundary to the south. Asher holds much of the land of eastern and central Galilee.

The inheritance of Dan (19:40–48)
The last tribe to receive an inheritance is Dan, the descendants of one of Jacob's sons born to Rachel's maidservant Bilhah (Genesis 30:1–6). Although the exact boundaries of Danite land are not provided, they can be established from the territories already given to the other tribes. Dan's location is west of the tribe of Benjamin, between Ephraim in the north and Judah in the south. It includes the coastal region from the Sorek Brook in the south to the Yarkon River in the north; of course, the Mediterranean Sea serves as its western border.

According to Judges 1:34, 'The Amorites pressed the people of Dan back into the hill country, for they did not allow them to come down to the plain.' Because of this solid resistance, the Danites mobilized and migrated to the very northern limits of the land of promise. They then captured the city of Leshem/ Dan, and settled in the region. This migration is discussed and described in detail in Judges 18.

The final allotment: Joshua (19:49–50)

As the distribution of land in Canaan began with a parcel being granted to an individual—that is Caleb (14:6–15)—so now it ends with the giving of an allotment to an individual, namely Joshua. This frames the entire affair of the allotment of the land in Canaan: the two former spies who had given a minority report to Moses now receive some of the land that they had scouted (Numbers 13).

Joshua is given the city of Timnath-serah; he had asked for it, and the Lord agreed that he should have it. The name of the city significantly means 'an extra, or "excess", portion', and that is exactly what Joshua receives. The city also goes by the name of Timnath-heres: it is here that Joshua later dies and is buried (24:30; Judges 2:9). Timnath-serah is located in the highlands of Ephraim in the southern hills of Samaria. No major city is near it: Aphek lies thirteen miles to the north-west and Bethel is ten miles to the south-east. The fact that Joshua's inheritance lies so far from the power centres of the day perhaps indicates that his time of leadership is coming to a close. Timnath-serah may be a retirement village!

Conclusion (19:51)

This summary verse indicates that the leadership of Israel act precisely on the commands of God regarding the allotment of the land of Canaan (see 14:1–2).

Points to ponder

1. A call to diligence as soldiers of Christ

In chapter 18:3 Joshua accuses the Israelites of being slack in taking possession of, and settling in, the land of Canaan. Due diligence is required of each tribe. All believers are called to be good soldiers of Christ and to be diligent in the Christian life and walk. The apostle Peter tells the church, 'Therefore, brothers, be all the more diligent to make your calling and election sure, for if you practise these qualities you will never fall' (2 Peter 1:10).

This reminds me of a story regarding the excavations at Pompeii. For years archaeologists have been uncovering the remains of that city, which was destroyed by the ash and lava of a devastating volcano. Researchers have discovered much evidence of people attempting to flee the catastrophe, and some individuals are permanently 'frozen' in a running position. But one man did not run. Burgess records that 'At the city gate was found a skeleton of a Roman guard. There he had remained, both hands clutched about his weapon, while the very ground on which he stood trembled and the fiery ashes were gradually burying him; after these many centuries, he was found at his post of duty.' That is true diligence. We as Christians are to be good soldiers of Christ, and we are to stand at our post, no matter what may come.

In 1724 Isaac Watts wrote the following hymn, with the title, 'Am I a Soldier of the Cross?':

Am I a soldier of the cross,
A foll'wer of the Lamb,
And shall I fear to own his cause,
Or blush to speak his name?

Must I be carried to the skies
On flow'ry beds of ease,
While others fought to win the prize,
And sailed through bloody seas?

Are there no foes for me to face?
Must I not stem the flood?
Is this vile world a friend of grace,
To help me on to God?

Sure, I must fight if I would reign:
Increase my courage, Lord;
I'll bear the toil, endure the pain,
Supported by thy Word.

2. Every true Christian will share in the inheritance of God's people
M. Wouldstra has pointed out that some of the material in chapters 18–19 repeats information already given in earlier chapters.[4] For example, he notes that the distinct inheritance of the Levites in 18:7 simply echoes what had previously been said about them in 13:14 and 14:4. Also, the assignment of the land in Transjordan to the tribes mentioned in 18:7 recounts earlier material from 13:8–32. Wouldstra comments:

> This is not needless redundancy but proceeds from the writer's thematic interest in the twelve tribe scheme and in the unity of Israel as it participates equally in the Conquest (cf. 1:12–18) and as it shows alike in the distribution of the promised land.[5]

This should remind us that all believers share alike in the heavenly inheritance. The apostle Paul says, 'Henceforth there is laid up for me the crown of righteousness, which the Lord, the righteous judge, will award to me on that Day, and not only to me but also to all who have loved his appearing' (2 Timothy 4:8). And, again, 'The Spirit himself bears witness with our spirit that we are children of God, and if children, then heirs—heirs of God and fellow heirs with Christ, provided we suffer with him in order that we may also be glorified with him' (Romans 8:16-17). For, finally, 'There is neither Jew nor Greek, there is neither slave nor free, there is neither male nor female, for you are all one in Christ Jesus. And if you are Christ's, then you are Abraham's offspring, heirs according to promise' (Galatians 3:28-29). Every Christian is an heir! All of true Israel shall receive the inheritance!

22

Cities of refuge

Please read Joshua 20:1–9

T he granting of the tribal inheritances is not the end of the allotment of land to the Israelites. There are still two more allocations that Joshua needs to make: first, the appointment of cities of refuge (chapter 20), and, secondly, the assignment of cities and pasturage to the Levites (chapter 21). The six asylum cities appointed in chapter 20 are also named as Levitical cities in chapter 21. The text, however, deals with the appointments separately, and therefore we shall do the same.

Asylum cities (20:1–3)

God now commands Joshua to tell the Israelites to appoint cities of refuge, or asylum. At Mount Sinai the Lord had said that such places would be appointed when Israel entered the land of promise (Exodus 21:12–14). That injunction is given in greater detail in Numbers 35:6–34. In the present chapter we see the fulfilment of those two passages as the Israelites designate the specific cities to serve as cities of asylum.

The purpose of an asylum city is to provide a place of refuge for someone who kills another person 'without intent or unknowingly'. He is to receive protection from 'the avenger of blood'.

> The term translated here as 'avenger' is the Hebrew word *gō'ēl* which actually refers to a kinsman-redeemer. The *gō'ēl* is one who delivers his relatives from danger and difficult situations (cf. Deuteronomy 25:5–10; Ruth 3:13). One of the duties of a *gō'ēl* is blood vengeance; if someone killed his relative then the *gō'ēl* was to reply in kind.[1]

The Lord simply does not allow blood retaliation without a trial, and so he provides places for the killer to run to until a trial can be held.

If one person kills another inadvertently he may run for safety to one of the cities of refuge. When he arrives there, he is to stand in front of the city gate. The elders, who often assembled at the gate of a city in Old Testament times (Ruth 4:1–2), will listen to the killer as he makes his case to be allowed entrance to the city (20:4).[2] The elders are, in a sense, the gatekeepers of the cities of asylum. Apparently the manslayer must convince the elders that his killing was without intent and accidental. If he succeeds, then the elders will allow him into the city and give him a place of residence.

If the avenger of blood tracks the killer to a city of asylum, then the elders will not deliver up the manslayer to him (20:5). The killer will be protected until the time of his trial.

Verse 6 is confusing unless it is read in the light of Numbers 35; the verse is a summary of a much larger section that appears in that earlier text (Numbers 35:25–29). The central focus of the passage is that if the killer is taken to trial and is found innocent, then he will live in the city of refuge until the death of the current high priest. The death of the high priest signals an amnesty: the killer may return to his home and the *gō'ēl* is released from his obligation of vengeance. There are various interpretations of why this is so. Some argue that the death of the high priest signifies the end of an old era and the dawning of a new one. Others believe that it is parallel to the amnesty granted to prisoners at the accession of a new king in the ancient Near East. Yet others believe that the death of the high priest is a form of expiation; as Harrison states, 'The death of the high priest was interpreted as an atonement for the offence of manslaughter.'[3]

Appointment of six cities of refuge (20:7–8)
In obedience to God's command the Israelites 'set apart' six cities as cities of asylum: three are in Canaan and three are in Transjordan. The order of the appointments in Canaan is: Kedesh in the north, Shechem in the central area and Hebron in the south. The arrangement is inverted in Transjordan; the names of the cities are given in the opposite direction: Bezer in the south, Ramoth in the central area and Golan in the north. This inversion is a literary technique that indicates that the whole of the land settled by Israel is covered and everyone has access to one of the cities of refuge. These cities are also widely spaced out so that a manslayer does not have to travel too far to seek asylum.

Law for the native and the sojourner (20:9)
The laws of asylum apply not only to the native Israelite, but

also to the 'stranger' who sojourns in Israel. A 'stranger', or 'sojourner', is a social status that ranks between a native of the land and a foreigner. A 'stranger' is an alien who lives and works among the native Israelites. The legal position of a 'stranger' is at best tenuous throughout the ancient Near East. Privileges are dependent solely on the hospitality of the natives of the country concerned.

According to Israelite law, the stranger is to be treated with great respect and with due process under the law. He is subject to the laws of Hebrew society (see, e.g., Exodus 12:19,48–49; 20:10; 23:12), and he also reaps the privileges of them (see Leviticus 16:29). And the reason he is to be dealt with in such a compassionate manner is as follows: 'You shall treat the stranger who sojourns with you as the native among you, and you shall love him as yourself, for you were strangers in the land of Egypt: I am the LORD your God' (Leviticus 19:34). Thus, with regard to the cities of refuge, the stranger has access to this zone of protection in the same way as the native Israelite.

Points to ponder

1. The death of the high priest as atonement
Even if a manslayer is found innocent of intentional murder, the *gōʾēl* still appears to be under an obligation to avenge the blood of his deceased relative. At this point the killer may live freely in a city of refuge without any threat or danger from the avenger of blood; he will not live in fear of reprisal. It is not until the death of the high priest that all is set right again: the manslayer may return home and the avenger of blood is released from his obligation of vengeance. Although not all interpreters agree, it does seem that the death of the high priest is a type of ransom

in which his death atones for 'the blood shed and satisfies the claims of justice'.[4]

If this interpretation is correct, then it provides a wonderful picture of the work of our High Priest, Christ Jesus! As the author of Hebrews says, 'For it was indeed fitting that we should have such a high priest ... He has no need, like those high priests, to offer sacrifices daily, first for his own sins and then for those of the people, since he did this once for all when he offered up himself' (Hebrews 7:26–27). Indeed, Jesus was 'a merciful and faithful high priest in the service of God, to make propitiation for the sins of the people'! (Hebrews 2:17).

2. The sanctity of human life

God takes seriously the crime of murder. In fact, it requires capital punishment (Genesis 9:6; Exodus 20:13; 21:23–25). Yet, as I wrote elsewhere:

> God also institutes statutes that help to determine whether a man is indeed guilty of premeditated murder. Decisions regarding guilt or innocence in the matter of crime are not left to chaos and pandemonium. Thus, God requires that there be a fair trial and that reputable witnesses be heard in the case. Only the person who wilfully, intentionally and deliberately kills another is to be executed. And the punishment of the guilty one is not arbitrary, nor is it for mere vengeance, but it is 'the due process of moral providence', as J. A. Motyer puts it. God is just, and he is the one who sets the standards for what is moral or immoral.[5]

These principles have not changed for today; human life is still sacred and it still needs to be preserved. Life in the image of

God is highly valued, and the unlawful taking of it incurs God's justice.

3. God's mercy extends to those who were once 'far off'

The laws of refuge apply not only to native Israelites, but also to the stranger who sojourns in the land (20:9). This demonstrates the breadth of God's mercy, so that even those foreigners who are not included in the covenant experience the privilege and protection of God's grace. Even here in the book of Joshua we witness God's compassion to non-Israelites; that mercy is clearly manifest earlier in the book with the deliverance of the Canaanite Rahab and her family. Such a tenderness is then found in full bloom in the New Testament, in which there 'is neither Jew nor Greek, there is neither slave nor free, there is neither male nor female, for you are all one in Christ Jesus' (Galatians 3:28). And, indeed, 'now in Christ Jesus you who once were far off have been brought near by the blood of Christ. For he himself is our peace, who has made us both one ...' (Ephesians 2:13–14).

23

Levitical cities and pasture lands

Please read Joshua 21:1–45

A t Mount Sinai the Lord set apart the tribe of Levi to oversee and to care for the religious, ceremonial activity of the people of Israel. That segregation of the Levites includes many ministerial tasks: they are given the work of assembling the tabernacle, taking it down and carrying it (Numbers 1:50–51). They are to guard and to protect the furnishings of the tabernacle, and to defend it against any incursions from unauthorized persons (Numbers 3:5–8).

Part of the tribe of Levi is the priesthood of Israel. A good adage to remember in this matter is that 'Not all Levites are priests, but all priests are Levites.' The Levitical priests have the duty to superintend the entire sacrificial system of Israel, as well as 'to distinguish between the holy and the common, and between the unclean and the clean, and ... to teach the people of Israel all the statutes that the LORD has spoken to them by Moses' (Leviticus 10:10-11).

Because the Levites have been set apart to the ritual labours of the holy things, they receive no land inheritance. The other tribes of Israel are to provide for the physical sustenance of the Levites: 'And you shall not neglect the Levite who is within your towns, for he has no portion or inheritance with you' (Deuteronomy 14:27). One of the ways that the tribes are to care for the Levites is by furnishing them with cities to live in and pasture lands for their animals. In the present chapter, the Levites ask for these cities and lands that have been promised to them by the Lord.

It is right and good that the church should take care of the material needs of its pastors and church leaders. The old saying of a congregation about its minister, 'Lord, you keep him humble, and we'll keep him poor,' is downright sinful and dastardly. Rather, it is true that 'The labourer deserves his wages' (1 Timothy 5:18, where Paul is quoting Jesus' words in Luke 10:7). As the Levites, who function as the spiritual leaders of Israel, have earthly needs—houses to live in and pastures for their flocks—so too pastors, evangelists, missionaries and other ministry workers have material needs. We in the church, the whole church—all the tribes!—are to care for them!

The claim of the Levites (21:1-3)

After the whole land of Canaan has been allotted to the tribes of Israel, the leaders of the tribe of Levi approach the principal authorities in Israel: the latter are Eleazer, the high priest, Joshua, the covenant mediator, and the leaders of the other tribes. They meet at Shiloh, and there the Levitical leaders make a request. They ask for cities to live in and adjoining pasture lands for their flocks and herds (21:2). This petition does not come out of the blue, but is based upon the very commands of God given to Moses before Israel crossed the Jordan River and conquered the land of Canaan. In Numbers 35:2 the Lord told Moses, 'Command the people of Israel to give to the Levites some of the inheritance of their possession as cities for them to dwell in. And you shall give to the Levites pasture lands around the cities.' At Shiloh, the Levites are demanding that Israel honour this command of God.

The Levitical cities are to be distributed throughout the Israelite territory in Canaan and Transjordan. No tribe is exempt from providing cities and land to the Levites. This widespread allocation is a fulfilment of Jacob's prophecy about Levi in Genesis 49:7: 'I will divide them in Jacob and scatter them in Israel.' There is a positive aspect to the wide dispersal of the Levitical cities: one of the primary tasks of the Levitical priesthood is defined in Leviticus 10:11: 'to teach the people of Israel all the statutes that the LORD has spoken to them by Moses'. By being dispersed throughout the entire Israelite territory, the Levites are then able to minister to all Israel.

The lots are cast (21:4–7)

This section sets out the number of cities that each tribe is to donate to the clans of the Levites. There are three Levitical clans: the Kohathites, the Gershonites and the Merarites. The apportionment of the Israelite cities is to be done by lots (21:4).

The Kohathite clans receive a total of twenty-three cities (21:4–5). Thirteen cities from the inheritance of the tribes of Judah, Simeon and Benjamin are designated for the priestly descendants of the Levites. And, then, ten cities from the lands of Ephraim, Dan and the half-tribe of Manasseh (in Canaan) are granted to the non-priestly Kohathites. The priestly Kohathites are located in the south of Canaan, and the non-priestly Kohathites are in central Canaan.

The Gershonite clan acquires thirteen cities, and these are found in the tribal territories of Issachar, Asher, Naphtali and the half-tribe of Manasseh (in Transjordan). The Gershonite holdings are thus located in the northern regions of Canaan.

The Merarites receive twelve cities in the tribal properties of Reuben, Gad and Zebulun. The first two tribes are located east of the Jordan River in Transjordan, and the last is in Galilee, just west of the Sea of Galilee.

The total number of cities allotted to the Levites is forty-eight, and they are widely dispersed throughout the entire Israelite area of settlement.

Naming the cities of the priestly Kohathites (21:8–19)

The biblical writer now names the specific cities which are granted to the Levites according to their clans. Nine towns from Judah and Simeon are presented to the priestly Kohathites: Hebron, Libnah, Jattir, Eshtemoa, Holon, Debir, Ain, Juttah and Beth-shemesh. Hebron is dealt with at greater length than the other cities because it had originally been consigned to Caleb (14:13). An important distinction is now made: the Kohathites receive the city and its pasture lands, but Caleb gets the open fields and the villages in the region of Hebron. Hebron is also a 'city of refuge for the manslayer' (21:13). Indeed, the cities of asylum are all designated as Levitical cities (21:13,21,27,32,36,38).

Naming the cities of the non-priestly Kohathites (21:20–26)

Ten cities are then allotted to the non-priestly Kohathites.

They are: Shechem (one of the refuge cities), Gezer, Kibzaim, Beth-horon from Ephraim; Elteke, Gibbethon, Aijalon and Gath-rimmon in Dan; Taanach and Gath-rimmon in the half-tribe of Manasseh. The city of Taanach was not captured during the conquest (17:11–12); its inclusion here anticipates its subjugation by the Israelites at a later time (see Judges 5:19).

Naming the cities of the Gershonites (21:27–33)
The clan of Gershon receives thirteen cities. These are: Golan (a city of refuge), Beeshterah, Kishion, Daberath, Jarmuth, En-gannim, Mishal, Abdon, Helkath, Rehob, Kedesh (another city of refuge), Hammoth-dor and Kartan.

Naming the cities of the Merarites (21:34–40)
The Merarites are called in verse 34 'the rest of the Levites'. As far as their Levitical duties are concerned, the Merarites have the least important roles with reference to the holy objects of the tabernacle. Their principal task is merely to take care of the frame of the tabernacle structure (see Numbers 4:29–33). There is less sanctity attached to these duties than to those of the other two clans.

The Merarites are allotted the following twelve cities: Jokneam, Kartah, Dimnah, Nahalal, Bezer (a city of refuge), Jahaz, Kedemoth, Mephaath, Ramoth (another refuge city), Mahanaim, Heshbon and Jazer.

Summary of the Levitical cities (21:41–42)
These two verses bring to a conclusion the apportionment of the Levitical cities and their pasture lands 'in the midst' of Israel's territorial possessions. The number of Levitical cities totals forty-eight, and this is the figure that the Lord specified to Moses in Numbers 35:6. It ought to be underscored at this point

that the Levitical cities are not the possession of the Levites, but
the Levites merely live in them (and probably alongside other
Israelites). They do not receive an inheritance like the other
tribes because the Lord is their inheritance (13:14,33).

Summary of the entire allotment of the land (21:43–45)

These three verses serve as a general summary and conclusion to
the major section dealing with the division of the land covering
chapters 13:1–21:42. This summing up tells the reader that the
land of promise is a gift of God; three times the verb 'to give' is
used of the Lord's activity of bestowing the land on the people.
The divine gift of the land is also a fulfilment of a promise that
God had made repeatedly to the patriarchs (see Genesis 12:7;
13:15; 17:8; 28:13—and note the use of the verb 'to give' in each
instance).

In addition, God gives the people rest from their enemies as
he had earlier promised (see Exodus 33:14; Deuteronomy 3:20;
12:10; 25:19). The Lord also pledged earlier that no man would
be able to withstand them (literally, 'stand before them'—see
Deuteronomy 7:24; 11:25; Joshua 1:5). All of these 'good promises'
have been kept and, indeed, not one word of them has failed to
come to pass. God simply keeps all his promises to his people.

Points to ponder

1. Christians are sojourners on earth

Karl Gutbrod has made the intriguing suggestion that the
Levites actually have the status of sojourners in the land of
Israel.[1] Deuteronomy 18:6 lends support to that understanding;
the text discusses the issue of the Levite and 'where he lives'.
That verb, 'to live', or 'reside', is normally used of an alien or
sojourner in a foreign land.[2] The Levite's status as a sojourner

can be understood as a picture of every Israelite's true position on the earth. In other words, when an Israelite looks at a Levite he is to be reminded that, in reality, he is a pilgrim on the earth. In Psalm 119:19, the psalmist declares, for instance, that he is 'a sojourner on the earth'. David makes the same assertion when he says to the Lord, 'For I am a sojourner with you, a guest, like all my fathers' (Psalm 39:12). He then associates this idea with the covenant people as a whole when he prays to the Lord before all the assembly of Israel: 'For we are strangers before you and sojourners, as all our fathers were' (1 Chr. 29:15).

Christians too should be continually reminded that we are merely aliens and sojourners on this earth. We are to be and act like the fathers:

> These all died in faith, not having received the things promised, but having seen them and greeted them from afar, and having acknowledged that they were strangers and exiles on the earth. For people who speak thus make it clear that they are seeking a homeland ... they desire a better country, that is, a heavenly one (Hebrews 11:13–16; cf. 1 Peter 1:1,17).

We are, in a sense, like the Levites because we have no land inheritance here, but we anticipate 'an inheritance that is imperishable, undefiled, and unfading, kept in heaven for you' (1 Peter 1:4).

2. The future rest that awaits the Christian

Not only does the Lord fulfil his promise to Israel by giving them 'the land that he swore to give to their fathers' (21:43), but he also gives them 'rest on every side' (21:44). As Christians we ought to anticipate and look longingly for the heavenly land inheritance and, moreover, to have great expectation of our eternal, heavenly rest. Richard Baxter, a Puritan pastor and author, wrote a book on this subject called *The Saints' Everlasting Rest*. He defines the Christian's future rest as:

> ... the end and perfection of motion. The saint's rest here in question is the most happy estate of a Christian, having obtained the end of his course; or, it is the perfect, endless fruition of God, by the perfected saints, according to the measure of their capacity, to which their souls arrive at death; and both soul and body most fully, after the resurrection and final judgement.[3]

The reality of a future land of rest also gives the Christian strength to carry on in this world. Baxter comments that when one looks heavenward, then things on earth take their proper place:

> Thy graces will be mighty, and active, and victorious; and the daily joy which is thus fetched from heaven, will be thy strength. Thou wilt be as one that standeth on the top of an exceeding high mountain; he looks down upon the world as if it were quite below him. How small do the fields and woods and countries seem to him? Cities and towns seem but little spots. Thus despicably wilt thou look on all things here below ... Men's threatening will be no terror to thee, nor the honours of this world any strong enticement. Temptations will be more harmless, having lost their strength, and afflictions less grievous, as having lost their sting; and every mercy will be better known and relished.[4]

Part 4:
The serving (22:1–24:33)

24

The altar

Please read Joshua 22:1–34

This chapter begins the final section of the book of Joshua. The opening section (1:1–5:12) describes the scene of Israel crossing into the land of Canaan; the second division (5:13–12:24) narrates the conquest of the land; and the third part (13:1–21:45) recounts the allocation of the land to the various tribes of Israel. This final section (22:1 –24:33) deals primarily with the unity of the tribes of Israel and the covenant renewal that takes place at Shechem. One of the principal questions of unity in these chapters is: who will Israel serve, now that they have secured the land of promise? Will they together serve the Lord who brought them out from the land of Egypt?

The question of fidelity is centre-stage in Joshua chapter 22. The nine and a half western tribes are stirred by the apparent treachery and apostasy of the two and a half eastern tribes. The eastern tribes construct an altar that appears to the western tribes to be a rival to the altar in the tabernacle at Shiloh. The building of such a structure is against Torah law (see Deuteronomy 12:13-14). In response, the western tribes take up arms. War, however, does not ensue because the western tribes misunderstand the purpose of the altar by the Jordan.

Some commentators argue that the western tribes are to blame for the situation because they resort to arms too quickly. They rush to make war.[1] I would disagree with that conclusion, and I would rather see the western tribes as responding passionately and appropriately to what appears to be an unauthorized worship site. A rogue monument like this altar could easily disrupt the covenantal unity and fidelity of Israel and, therefore, immediate action is required. In addition, the western tribes show some restraint. They do not attack immediately, but they send a delegation to meet with the leaders of the eastern tribes. This is, indeed, the right course of action.

The church today could use some of this passion against false teaching and apostasy in the church. We are very tolerant of aberrant means of worship and practice. Obviously we need not be vicious, but we do need to guard the true worship of God. Saint Augustine provides the proper balance when he says, 'Love men, slay error; without pride be bold in the truth, without cruelty fight for the truth.'[2]

Obedience of the Transjordanian tribes (22:1-6)
With the allocation of the land of Canaan complete, Joshua summons to Shiloh the two and a half tribes who are to settle in Transjordan. There he praises them for their obedience. He tells them that they have 'obeyed' the commands of Joshua (22:2) and they have 'kept' the directives of both Moses and the Lord (22:2-3). They have simply been faithful to their word which they gave

to the leaders in the wilderness (Numbers 32:25–27) and on the banks of the Jordan River (1:16–18). Joshua then releases them from any further obligation to their brothers in Canaan with regard to the conquest of the land. The two and a half tribes may now return to the east side of the Jordan River; Joshua tells them to 'go to your tents' (22:4). They had left their families and flocks in Transjordan in an unsettled existence (Deuteronomy 3:19), and now they may go back to their 'tents' and begin to settle their possession.

Joshua encourages the two and a half tribes to continue in obedience according to the commandments of God. The very basis of their existence is the Word of God. This is certainly true of all God's people throughout history. For instance, the *Westminster Shorter Catechism* asks and answers the following two questions:

> *Question 2:* What rule hath God given to direct us how we may glorify and enjoy him?

> *Answer:* The Word of God, which is contained in the Scriptures of the Old and New Testaments, is the only rule to direct us how we may glorify and enjoy him.

> *Question 3:* What do the Scriptures principally teach?

> *Answer:* The Scriptures principally teach, what man is to believe concerning God, and what duty God requires of man.

Joshua then summarizes the people's duty to obey God's law by employing five verbs in a staccato fashion: to 'love', to 'walk', to 'keep', to 'cling' and to 'serve'. These verbs underscore one idea—namely, that the tribes in Transjordan must continue to demonstrate fidelity to the Word of God.

Finally, Joshua 'blessed' the two and a half tribes and ordered them to return to Transjordan. The verb 'to bless' in Hebrew culture means to confer, or to endue with power for, success, prosperity and longevity. It signifies that the recipient is being empowered to exceptional fecundity (see Genesis 9:1,7; 12:2, etc.). On that note, the Transjordanian tribes depart from Shiloh and go on their way to the land of their possession.

An aside (22:7-9)

These three verses provide an addendum to the commands that Joshua gave to the Transjordanian tribes at Shiloh. Joshua directs these tribes to share the plunder amassed in Canaan during the conquest with their brethren. This appears to be a common expectation of the time. For example, when the Israelites defeated the Midianites during the conquest of Transjordan, the Lord told them to 'divide the plunder into two parts between the warriors who went out to battle and all the congregation' (Numbers 31:27; cf. 1 Samuel 30:24-25). Apparently the Israelites seized significant spoil during the conquest of Canaan (see 8:2,27; 11:14). As a result, the two and a half tribes return to their land possession with 'much wealth' (22:8).

Building an altar (22:10-12)

On their travels back to Transjordan, the warriors from the two and a half tribes stop near the Jordan River. There, on the west side of the river 'in the land of Canaan', they build 'an altar of imposing size' (22:10). When the other tribes hear about the altar, their soldiers gather at the headquarters at Shiloh in order to make war against the eastern tribes (22:12).

What is it about this act that causes such a demonstrative military reaction on the part of the western tribes? Why do they respond by mustering their troops? First, the tribes west of the Jordan may perhaps view the building of the altar 'on the side that belongs to the people of Israel' (22:11) as an incursion into their territory and inheritance. In other words, the two and a half tribes belong on the eastern side of the Jordan River; why are they building a huge altar on the west side of the river? In addition, as we shall see in subsequent verses, the tribes in Canaan believe that this building activity is a form of apostasy and religious rebellion. Therefore, they muster themselves for battle.

Confrontation (22:13–20)

Prior to any military confrontation, the nine and a half tribes send a delegation to hold a council with the Transjordanian tribes. They send ten leaders, one from each tribe, and Phinehas at their head. Phinehas is a threatening figure in this context because he is most famous for his violent dealings with Israelite idolaters (see Numbers 25:1–9). Phinehas, as a priest, has a great zeal for the purity of Israel's worship. The appointment of Phinehas at the head of this delegation would not have been lost on the two and a half tribes.

The delegation arrives in Gilead, which is part of the land inheritance of the eastern half of the tribe of Manasseh, and they confront the tribes who had built the altar. They accuse them of 'breach of faith', an allegation of treachery and unfaithfulness (22:16). In Joshua 7:1 the author employs the same word to describe Israel's sin in the episode concerning Achan. The delegation directly indicts the Transjordanian tribes of 'rebellion against the LORD' (22:16). In what sense is the building of an altar rebellious? What do the western tribes believe the eastern tribes have done by the building activity?

The western tribes believe that the altar is meant to be a rival to the altar of burnt offering in the tabernacle at Shiloh. Thus, the accusation is clear: the Transjordanian tribes are setting up 'an altar other than the altar of the LORD our God' (22:19). The reality is that 'Sacrifices are to be offered to God, and his worship is to be centralized, in only one place—"the" place—that is, the sanctuary (be it the tabernacle or the temple).'[3] So, in the eyes of the western tribes, the eastern tribes are committing apostasy; they are deserting and abandoning the Torah.

The western tribes are also concerned about communal liability (22:18). If the eastern tribes 'turn away' from following the Lord, then 'he will be angry', or irate, against all Israel. The reality is that the actions of some members of the covenant community will indeed affect the entire body (cf. Numbers 25; Joshua 7). In fact, the delegation warns the eastern tribes not to rebel in this way and thus 'make us as rebels by building ... an altar' (22:19). All Israel may suffer for the sins of the few, or even of the one. Just as we saw in the story of Achan, he 'did not perish alone for his iniquity' (22:20). Here, the western tribes assert their corporate responsibility in order to prevent such suffering.

Response of the eastern tribes (22:21–29)

The two and a half tribes now try to defend their actions and to demonstrate that the accusation of treachery is unfounded. They argue that they have not apostatized. They begin their defence with a confession of faith: 'The Mighty One, God, the LORD! The Mighty One, God, the LORD!' (22:22). The repetition of this creed underscores the orthodoxy of the eastern tribes—

they are followers of the one God, Yahweh, the God of Israel. They claim that they have not gone astray or rejected the true religion of Israel by constructing this altar by the Jordan. In fact, they take an oath on the matter: if they have become heterodox, they ask not to be spared by the armies of Israel! (22:22).

The truth is that the eastern tribes did not construct the altar for sacrificial offerings (22:23). Instead, they intended it as a 'witness', or a physical symbol, to serve as a reminder to all Israel (22:27). The two and a half tribes built the altar in fear that future generations of Israel might forget that they are part of the Israelite covenant people, or that they might in fact be treated as second-class citizens in Israel, and not as true worshippers of the Lord (22:24–25). The Jordan River is a natural barrier and divider; the eastern tribes are simply concerned that their progeny will one day be shunned in Israel.

The eastern tribes recognize the problem they have caused: the altar they have built is an exact 'copy' of the altar of burnt offering in the tabernacle at Shiloh (22:28). However, that is mere appearance: these tribes have no intention 'to offer burnt offerings or grain offerings or peace offerings on it' (22:23). It is merely to serve as a 'witness', or a memorial, a monument, that they too are part of the covenant people. Thus these tribes flatly and directly deny that they are rebelling against, or turning away from, the Lord (22:29); in fact, the opposite is true!

Reply of the delegation (22:30–31)
The explanation given by the eastern tribes satisfies the delegation of the western tribes; in fact, 'it was good in their eyes'. Phinehas declares that the Transjordanian tribes have not committed a rebellious act. Actually, the truth of the explanation saved the western tribes from acting rashly by

making war on the eastern tribes. War would have been uncalled for, and all Israel would have suffered major consequences of it. When Phinehas proclaims that the eastern tribes 'have delivered the people of Israel from the hand of the LORD', he means that the explanation given by the eastern tribes has diverted all Israel from disaster.

Response of the western tribes (22:32–34)
The delegation now returns to Shiloh to present its findings. When the western tribes hear the account of the meeting, they respond in the same manner as the delegation did: the report 'was good in the eyes' of the people (22:33; cf. 22:30). The immediate result of the communication is that it stops all talk of, and preparation for, war. The time of danger has now passed.

The final event in this episode is the naming of the altar by the eastern tribes (22:34). The name of the altar is disputed by biblical commentators because the first line of the verse literally reads, 'And the sons of Reuben and the sons of Gad called to the altar.' No name is apparently provided for the altar, and some believe that perhaps the name has dropped out of the text. That is why a translation like the English Standard Version adds the name 'Witness' to the text. Other interpreters argue that, in fact, the last line of the verse—'it is a witness between us that the LORD is God'—is actually the name of the altar. That may be the case because in Scripture we sometimes see altars, or monuments, with names that consist of short sentences (see Exodus 17:15; Judges 6:24).

This monument is the sixth one built by the people of Israel in the land of Canaan during the time of the conquest and land allocation (see 4:20; 7:26; 8:28–29; 8:30–32; 10:27). These all bear witness to the covenantal unity of the tribes of Israel.

Points to ponder

1. Faithfulness and obedience to God's Word are to be commended

At the outset of chapter 22 we read that Joshua commends the two and a half tribes for their obedience and fidelity to the word they gave to Moses. They had promised that they would go to battle in Canaan with the other tribes (Numbers 32:27). Their word is their bond, and they have done as they pledged. So Joshua praises and blesses them.

Church leaders ought to extol and encourage the people of God when they are faithful and dutiful in their obedience to the Word of God. Preachers are very good at scolding their congregations from the pulpit for not keeping God's Word, but they are not as adept in reassuring them when they are obedient. For instance, in the three years of my present pastoral position I have preached only one sermon on tithing: it was during a series I was preaching on Philippians (the passage was Philippians 4:14–19). In that sermon I did not urge my people *to* tithe, but I commended them *for* their tithing. This congregation is a very giving community and, therefore, it did not need to be admonished but, rather, to be commended. And, in fact, that is the same way that Paul deals with the Philippian church in the passage I was preaching on.

2. A call to continued faithfulness to the Word of God

Joshua further encourages the eastern tribes to continue in their faithful walk in obedience to the Word of God. Scripture is the very basis and heart of their existence. The same is true for the people of God throughout the ages. For example, the third question of the *Westminster Larger Catechism* is: 'What is the word of God?' Its answer is, 'The holy scriptures of the Old and New Testament are the word of God, the only rule of faith and obedience.' A work called *The Testimony of the Seceders* (1736) puts it this way: 'The Word of God contained in the Scriptures of the Old and New Testaments is not only a sufficient rule, or a principal rule, but it is the only rule to direct us how we ought to glorify God and enjoy him.'

The Word of God is to be our daily meat and portion—that is, our very life-blood. Guthrie describes it well when he says that:

[The Word of God] is an armoury of heavenly weapons, a laboratory of infallible medicines, a mine of exhaustless wealth. It is a guide-book for every road, a chart for every sea, a medicine for every malady, a balm for every wound. Rob us of our Bible, and our sky has lost its sun, and in the best of other books we have naught but the glimmer of twinkling stars. It is the wealth of the poor, blessing poverty with the contentment which makes it rich. It is the shield of wealth, protecting the few that are rich against the many that are poor. It may be compared to the skies, which hold at once the most blessed and the most baneful elements—soft dews to bathe the opening rose, and bolts that rend the oak asunder.[4]

3. Resolving conflict in the church

There is a good end to the conflict between the tribes of Israel in the episode concerning the altar. The story is a good example of conflict resolution in the church. The western tribes send a delegation to make certain that they properly understand the purpose and intent of the eastern tribes in building the altar. This action generally reminds us of Jesus' teaching in Matthew 18 with regard to discord in the church:

If your brother sins against you, go and tell him his fault, between you and him alone. If he listens to you, you have gained your brother. But if he does not listen, take one or two others along with you, that every charge may be established by the evidence of two or three witnesses. If he refuses to listen to them, tell it to the church. And if he refuses to listen even to the church, let him be to you as a Gentile and a tax collector (Matthew 18:15–17).

25

Joshua's charge

Please read Joshua 23:1–16

In the mid-sixteenth century, Jane Grey ascended the throne of England, but she was quickly deposed and then executed by beheading. She was a Christian, a Protestant, and one who was steeped in the Bible and the catechisms. Kneeling at the scaffold, she recited the fifty-first psalm in its entirety— that is, David's great psalm of contrition. Then she turned and witnessed to those in attendance regarding the salvation that one can have through the blood of Jesus. The executioner was so moved that he asked Jane Grey to forgive him. She put her head on the block, and called out in a clear, strong voice, 'Lord, into thy hands I commend my spirit!' Lady Jane Grey was sixteen years old.

After her arrest, Lady Jane Grey was imprisoned in the Tower of London. The night before her beheading she wrote a note in the back of her Greek New Testament urging her sister to become a Christian. Jane Grey was going through the crucible, yet she responded to it by evangelizing her sister. What courage, willpower and strength to face even the ultimate sacrifice!

At the end of Joshua's life, he gives a final charge to the leadership of Israel. His call to them centres on the command to 'be very strong' (23:6); this is the same command that God gave to Joshua at the beginning of the book (1:6–9). The summons to strength, courage and obedience to the Word of the Lord thus brackets the narrative of the book. It is a frame that underscores the primary purpose and goal of the book. Israel is required to stand firm and fast for the Lord, and the people are not to waver in obedience, no matter what hurdles they might face.

The summons (23:1–5)

The text begins with the phrase, 'A long time afterwards'. This is an idiomatic expression in Hebrew for an undesignated period of time. We are not certain how much time has elapsed between the end of chapter 22 and the beginning of chapter 23. The statement that Joshua 'was old and well advanced in years' (23:1) is not particularly helpful in dating the passage because the same thing was said of him prior to the allotment of the land (see 13:1). It has been argued that perhaps as much as a quarter of a century has passed since Israel first crossed the Jordan River by this point in the story—'assuming that Joshua was similar in age to Caleb at the beginning of the conquest (who was nearing 80 ... [see comments on 11:16–18]), and in view of Joshua's age of 110 at death (24:29).'[1] This, however, is speculative.

Joshua summons the leadership of Israel to meet with him. The location of this assembly is uncertain. The covenant-renewal ceremony in the last chapter of the book occurs at Shechem, but no location is given for Joshua's charge in chapter

23. It probably takes place at Shiloh, since this is the last Israelite headquarters mentioned in the book prior to the present account (see 22:12).

Joshua begins his charge to Israel by reminding them of the foundational truth that it is the Lord 'who has fought for you' (23:3). The Israelites are where they are because of God's work; indeed, 'The LORD is a man of war' (Exodus 15:3). This is a recurring theme throughout the entire conquest (Deuteronomy 1:30; 3:22; 20:4; Joshua 23:10). Joshua also reminds the leaders that not only has Israel conquered the land by the power of God, but it has been assigned to them by the Lord (23:4). And, although not every inch of the land has been seized, and some of the peoples remain in the land, God will continue to lead the charge against them (23:5).

What is Israel's duty? (23:6)
Although God fights on Israel's behalf, the people of God nevertheless have duties to perform. The people are, first of all, to 'be very strong'. This is a similar charge to the one that the Lord gave to Joshua at the beginning of the conquest; three times he said to Joshua, 'Be strong' (1:6–9). The Lord charges Joshua to be strong by 'being careful to do according to all the law that Moses my servant commanded you. Do not turn from it to the right hand or to the left ...' (1:7). This command quite closely parallels what we read in the present verse. These correspondences reflect a literary *inclusio*—that is, the two passages serve as book-ends to the narrative of Joshua. This *inclusio* underscores what is the central point to the entire book: Israel must be strong and vigilant to obey the Word of God!

Who will Israel serve? (23:7–11)
The greatest threat to Israel's keeping the Word of God comes

from the peoples who remain in the land of Canaan and the multiplicity of their gods. Verse 7 consists of five negative commands to Israel. First, the people of God are not to 'mix with', or, literally, 'not go in with', the peoples left in the land; they are not to covenant with them or make a treaty with them, or live peaceably with them. Mixing is dangerous business, and it often leads to idolatrous worship. Secondly, they are not to invoke 'the names' of the pagan gods—that is, to give allegiance to them. Thirdly, the Israelites are not to take an oath or 'swear by' the names of these pagan gods. Fourthly, they are not to 'serve' these gods. And, finally, they are not to 'bow down to them' or worship them. The last two negatives are reminiscent of the second commandment of the Decalogue, which says, 'You shall not bow down to them or serve them' (Exodus 20:5). This staccato list of negative commands has great clarity: Israel is to stay away from the pagan gods.

On the contrary, the people of God are to 'cling' to the Lord (23:8). They are to grip and to cleave to him alone.[2] Indeed, why would they chase after other gods when it is 'the LORD your God who fights for you' (23:10) and 'no man has been able to stand before you'? (23:9). Therefore, Israel is to be very careful and diligent 'to love' the Lord, and him only! (23:11).

The consequences of serving other gods (23:12–13)

If Israel turns away from God, then dire and severe consequences will result. The people must not 'cling' to the nations (23:12). The verb 'to cling' is the same one used in verse 8; the contrast is obvious, posing the question: who will Israel 'cling' to? Will they cling to the Lord, or turn away and cling to the nations?

One form of clinging to the pagan nations is by inter-marrying with them. Such activity is strictly forbidden in the law (see Exodus 34:16; Deuteronomy 7:3–4). Intermarriage remains a constant and continuing threat to Israel in the land of Canaan throughout her history (see, e.g., 1 Kings 11:1–2). In addition, the end of verse 12 literally says that Israel is not 'to go in' with these pagan peoples; this is covenant language and it forbids Israel from making such treaty agreements. This prohibition is echoed in many passages of the law (see Exodus 23:32; 34:12; Deuteronomy 7:2).

The consequences of Israel's choosing to cling to the nations rather than to the Lord will be disastrous (23:13). First, Israel should know for certain and clearly that the Lord will stop dispossessing the nations from the land of Canaan. There is irony in this: if Israel wants to cling to the pagan nations, then God will allow those peoples to remain in the land of promise. But, in reality, they will not be a source of good to Israel. Indeed not! They will be, literally, 'a bird-trap', and 'a snare' and 'a scourge' and 'thorns in your eyes'. Ultimately, Israel will 'perish' from the land of promise if they persist in clinging to the nations. They will be driven into exile, and captivity will be their lot in a land far away from Canaan. Thus the Israelites will become like the nations they cling to, and they will receive the end that should have been the lot of the nations—namely, expulsion from the land of milk and honey. In other words, the nations will remain in the land of promise and the Israelites will be driven from it.

Joshua's final charge to the leaders (23:14–16)

Joshua tells the leadership of Israel that he is soon to die: he uses the Hebrew idiom, 'to go the way of all the earth' (23:14), to express his impending demise (see 1 Kings 2:2). And, because he will soon die, he gives this final testamentary address to the officers of the covenant people. He first reminds them of a truth that ought to be embedded in the very depths of their hearts: everything that God has promised to the children of Israel has come to pass (23:14). The text underscores this truth by saying, literally, 'Not one word has fallen from it.' The Lord is a God who keeps his word, even down to the very words themselves!

The leadership of Israel needs to understand that God is a promise keeper not only with regard to his blessings, but also to his threats (23:15). If Israel oversteps the bounds of the covenant by committing idolatry, then there *will* come a day of reckoning (23:16). The Lord *will* 'bring upon' Israel 'all the evil things'; these punishments are listed in Leviticus 26:14–39 and Deuteronomy 28:15–68. In the end, an idolatrous, covenant-breaking Israel *will* be driven out of the promised land quickly and decisively. This, of course, is what eventually befalls the people of God (see 2 Kings 17:7–20). God is true to his word.

Points to ponder

1. Christians are to be strong in life and in death

Christians are to stand fast and to be strong, no matter what circumstances they face in life. Whether it be life or death, joy or sorrow, mourning or dancing, the believer is to be strong and courageous in the Lord. Bunyan provides a good example in the second part of *The Pilgrim's Progress* when he describes the pilgrimage of Christian's wife and children to the celestial city. He tells of a Mr Standfast who is crossing the cold river of death:

Now there was a great calm at that time in the river; wherefore Mr Standfast, when he was about halfway in, stood a while and talked to his companions that had waited upon him thither; and he said, 'This river has been a terror to many; yea the thoughts of it have often frightened me. But now, methinks, 1 stand easy ... The waters indeed are to the palate bitter, and to the stomach cold, yet the thoughts of what 1 am going to and the convoy that wait for me on the other side, lie as a glowing coal at my heart. 1 see myself now at the end of my journey; my toilsome days are ended. 1 am going now to see that head which was crowned with thorns, and that face which was spit upon for me.

'1 have formerly lived by hearsay and faith, but now 1 go where 1 shall live by sight, and shall be with him in whose company 1 delight myself. 1 have loved to hear my Lord spoken of; and wherever 1 have seen the print of his shoe in the earth, there 1 have coveted to set my foot too... His voice to me has been most sweet; and his countenance 1 have more desired than they that have most desired the light of the sun. His words 1 did use to gather for my food, and for antidotes against my faintings ...'

Now while he was thus in discourse, his countenance changed; his strong man bowed under him, and after he had said, 'Take me, for 1 come unto Thee,' he ceased to be seen of them.

2. The source of our strength is the Word of God

Just like Israel, the standard of our strength and obedience is the Word of God. It is our authority in life and practice. The *Scots Confession* (1560) puts it this way: 'As we believe and confess the scriptures of God sufficient to instruct and make perfect the man of God, so do we affirm and avow their authority to be from God, and not to depend on men or angels.' The *Westminster Confession of Faith* (1642) agrees: 'The authority of the Holy Scripture, for which it ought to be believed, and obeyed, dependeth not on the testimony of any man, or church; but wholly upon God (who is truth itself) the author thereof: and therefore it is to be received, because it is the Word of God' (Chapter 1:4). The Bible is the only rule of faith and obedience.

The Scots' pastor Robert Murray M'Cheyne tells the following story regarding the strength given by the Word of God:

I shall never forget the story of a little girl in Belfast, in Ireland. She was at a Sabbath School, and gained a Bible as a prize for her good conduct. It became to her a treasure indeed. She was fed out of it. Her parents were wicked. She often read to them, but they became worse and worse. This broke Eliza's heart. She took to her bed and never rose again. She desired to see her teacher. When he came he said, 'You are not without a companion, my dear child,' taking up her Bible. 'No,' she replied:

Precious Bible! What a treasure
Does the Word of God afford!
All I want for life or pleasure,
Food and med'cine, shield and sword.
Let the world account me poor,
Having this, I ask no more.

She had scarcely repeated the lines when she hung back her head and died. Beloved children, this is the way Jesus feeds his flock. He is a tender, constant, Almighty Shepherd. If you become His flock, He will feed you all the way to glory.

3. The need to persevere
The Israelites persevered through the conquest, and they succeeded in capturing the land of Canaan. Now a much

harder and longer-lasting test remains: they are in the land for the long haul in order to complete the conquest and to live a settled existence. They must continue in fidelity to the Lord and they must stay true to his Word in order to retain the land. The conquest is only the beginning; now they must keep the inheritance that the Lord has given to them.

Perseverance in life is required of all believers. Spurgeon put it this way:

> Perseverance is the badge of true saints. The Christian life is not a beginning only in the ways of God, but also a continuance in the same as long as life lasts. It is with a Christian as it was with the great Napoleon: he said, 'Conquest has made me what I am, and conquest must maintain me.'

Many of the saints of the Bible did well in the most perilous times, yet they fell when the danger was over. Noah faced the flood with Christian character and courage, but soon afterwards he succumbed to immorality. David defeated all his enemies round about with godly daring, but he soon fell as he was at his ease in the palace and saw a woman bathing. Elijah was fearless when he confronted the prophets of Baal on Mount Carmel, but he quickly fled in fear and confusion when that event was over. Believers must stand fast over the long trek, whether it be during times of ease or times of peril.

Christians do have great encouragement in perseverance. Endurance in this life to the very end is the work of God in us. Paul tells the Philippian church, 'I am sure of this, that he who began a good work in you will bring it to completion at the day of Jesus Christ' (Philippians 1:6). The reality is that God does not promise us a journey without storms, but he does promise us that we will arrive at the port safely.

26

Second renewal of the covenant

Please read Joshua 24:1–28

The section we are about to consider is a covenant-renewal ceremony that takes place at the site of Shechem in the central highlands of Canaan. It has long been recognized that this passage is set up according to the structure of a common ancient Near-Eastern suzerain/vassal treaty:

In the ancient Near East, there existed two types or forms of covenant: those governing relationships between *equal* parties and those specifying relationships between *unequal* parties. The second type of covenant was between an overlord (the superior, also called a suzerain) and a vassal (the inferior party). Many of these covenants were between a king and his subjects. Within this form, the suzerain, as the more powerful party, took on most of the responsibility for the stipulations of the covenant. Although the vassal also had some obligations, because of limited capabilities and resources, he was not held accountable to the same extent and degree as the suzerain.[1]

Most of the treaty documents discovered in the ancient Near East through archaeology are Hittite covenants that come from the second millennium BC. Some covenant documents, from the Assyrians, Egyptians, Hittites and others, have been found that date to the first millennium BC. However, the covenant-renewal ceremony in Joshua 24 most closely resembles treaty documents of the second millennium BC from the Hittites.

A comparative study of the ceremony in Joshua 24:1–28 with extant Hittite covenant documents reveals many common features and elements. In addition, the order of the elements is closely matched between the two: preamble (24:2); historical prologue (24:3–13); stipulations (24:14–15); oath (24:16–18); sanctions (24:19–21); witnesses (24:22–24); and a statement of display (24:25–26). We will consider our passage according to these elements and their chronology in the text.

Introduction (24:1)

The geographical setting of the book now shifts to the site of Shechem. It is a city located in the central highlands of Canaan, and it sits at a major crossroads in the land. It lies between the mountains known as Gerizim and Ebal. Extensive excavations have taken place at Shechem, and they have revealed that it was an important centre of pagan worship in the Middle and Late Bronze Ages. Several large and important 'courtyard' temples from the Canaanite period were uncovered at the site. The book of Joshua does not recount the conquest of Shechem by the Israelites; perhaps it submitted peacefully. It is an important city in the inheritance of the tribe of Ephraim because it is designated both as a city of refuge (20:7) and as a Levitical city (21:21).

In our text, Joshua summons the people of Israel to Shechem; the leaders are apparently then called to the front of the gathering of the tribes. There the people, literally, 'stand themselves' before the Lord. It is likely that the ark and the tabernacle have been temporarily moved for this momentous occasion (see 24:26). The ark had been present at the covenant-renewal ceremony that had taken place at Mount Ebal and Mount Gerizim at the beginning of the conquest (8:30–35). Now it makes its appearance at the end of the conquest at another covenant-renewal ceremony.

Preamble (24:2)

Kline states that 'Ancient suzerainty treaties began with a preamble in which the speaker, the one who was declaring his lordship and demanding the vassal's allegiance, identified himself.'[2] Joshua begins his speech to Israel by declaring, 'Thus says the Lord.' He uses a common prophetic formula in the ancient Near East to preface the commands of a deity. It is an introductory idiom that signifies that the words which follow derive directly from the deity, and that they are not to be altered or changed in any way. The role of the prophet, such as Joshua, is to communicate that word without modification. In other words, this is God speaking and introducing himself as speaker.

The prophetic utterance of Joshua underscores the fact that he is a prophet like Moses. Moses had used the prophetic formula, 'Thus says the Lord', on numerous occasions (see, e.g., Exodus 5:1; 8:1; etc.). Joshua is in the prophetic line (see Deuteronomy 18:15–22).

Historical prologue (24:3–13)

'In ancient Near-Eastern treaties between two leaders, or between a suzerain and a vassal, the preamble is immediately followed by a section that surveys the history of the relationship between the two parties of the covenant.'[3] Beginning in the second half of verse 2 and continuing through verse 13, God, the suzerain, reviews the history of his relationship with Israel. It begins with the Lord's call of Abraham out of Mesopotamia to go to the land of Canaan. It continues with the multiplication of Abraham's progeny through his descendants Isaac, Jacob and Esau. The narrative then tells of the Egyptian bondage and how God delivered the people by means of plagues and the miracle at the Red Sea. The chronological history concludes with the wilderness wanderings, the conquest of Transjordan and the capture of the land of Canaan.

This survey places God at the very heart of Israel's history. In fact, the leading verb throughout this section is 'I gave'; it appears six times in verses 3 through 13, and that underscores the centrality of God to the unfolding redemptive history of Israel. It is God who is active, and history is playing out according to his will and decree.

The primary purpose of the historical prologue in a covenant is to establish historical justification for the continuance of the arrangement between the two parties. Especially in a suzerain/vassal treaty like the one we have here, the benefits of the covenant to the vassal in the past are often highlighted in order to evoke a sense of gratitude from him. Seeing how the suzerain has treated him in the past, the vassal should be thankful for, and agreeable to, the renewed ratification of the covenantal agreement. It should also give the vassal hope for the future.

Stipulations (24:14-15)

The next feature of a covenant is the stipulations of the treaty. These spell out the obligations that each party has under the terms of the oath. Often only the responsibilities of the vassal in respect to the suzerain are given in detail; the duties of the suzerain are often assumed, or taken for granted. On the vassal's side, Israel is, first, to 'fear' the Lord; this verb in Hebrew refers not to knee-knocking terror, but rather to an awe and wonder of God that lead to obedience and worship of him. The idea that Israel is to fear God in this way has been taught earlier in the book (see 4:24).

Secondly, Israel is required to 'serve' the Lord alone (24:14). This verb is a leading word (*Leitwort*), or keyword, in this section as it appears six times in these two verses. The big question in the covenant renewal is clear: who will Israel serve? Three options are stated by Joshua. Will Israel serve the ancestral gods of Mesopotamia (see 24:2), or the gods of Canaan where they now reside, or the Lord? Joshua, as covenant mediator, is a great example for the people as he declares that he and his household 'will serve the LORD' (24:15). Joshua's leadership prevails, for we read near the end of the book that 'Israel served the LORD all the days of Joshua, and all the days of the elders who outlived Joshua' (24:31). This is, indeed, a great legacy for Joshua!

Oath of allegiance (24:16-18)

Ancient Near-Eastern covenant documents often include an oath of obedience, or allegiance, on the part of the vassal. In these verses the people make an oral proclamation that they will not 'serve' other gods (24:16). Then they make a pledge of fidelity to God by announcing, '... we also will serve the LORD' (24:18). The reasoning of the people is clear and simple: the Lord has been faithful to them by delivering them out of Egypt, caring for them in the wilderness and dispossessing the pagan peoples out of the land of promise. God is true to his word and his promises; Israel responds by decisively rejecting the pagan gods and by clinging to the Lord. Thus they take an oath of loyalty to the Lord.

Sanctions (24:19–21)

Sanctions are often listed in ancient covenant documents. These are blessings and curses invoked on the vassal depending on whether or not he keeps the covenant. No sanctions are placed on the suzerain because it is assumed that he will keep his word and that he will be loyal and faithful to the covenant with Israel.

The central point of contention is whether or not Israel will stay true to the covenant. God will not condone apostasy. The curse for unfaithfulness is clear: if Israel turns from the Lord to serve pagan gods, then the Lord will turn upon Israel, harm them and consume them. Joshua confronts the people by saying that they are not able to keep the covenant, and their past history is proof of unfaithfulness. Certainly his point is that they cannot keep the covenant in and of themselves and in their own strength, but they must seek divine assistance. In addition, Joshua is not saying that the Lord is unforgiving to Israel. In reality, the Lord has shown time and again his longsuffering character towards the people's sin. What Joshua is proclaiming is that apostasy simply will not be condoned!

The people respond to Joshua's emphatic teaching by the reiteration of the oath that they had taken in verse 18. They are equally emphatic. They say, 'No,' but they will indeed 'serve the LORD'! (24:21). Israel's response to Joshua is immediate, spontaneous and unhesitating. This mere reassertion of the covenant oath makes one wonder whether or not Israel really takes to heart what Joshua had said to them. How deep is their commitment, really?

Witnesses (24:22–24)

A common element of an ancient Near-Eastern covenant is a witness clause. The suzerain calls on various things to testify to the validity of the covenant. In one Hittite treaty of the second millennium BC, the king, Mursilis, calls on the gods to bear witness to the covenant between himself and a vassal. He also invokes various parts of nature to testify to the oath: '... the mountains, the rivers, the springs, the great Sea, heaven and earth, the winds [and] the clouds ... let these be witnesses to this treaty and to the oath.'[4] When the God of the Bible makes a covenant with his people he also employs a variety of witnesses to it (see, for example, Deuteronomy 31:19,21,26; 32:46).

In the present setting, Joshua announces that the Israelites will be 'witnesses' against themselves. The Hebrews respond literally with one word: 'witnesses'. They are simply echoing Joshua's pronouncement with a one-word thunderclap.

To prove that they are truly convicted and committed, Joshua expects the Israelites to 'put away the foreign gods' among them and to cling only to the Lord. Some commentators believe that this refers to the idols still being worshipped by the nations remaining in the land of Canaan. It is more likely, however, that some idolatry is still being tolerated among the people of Israel, and this pagan worship needs to cease immediately. Israel's accession to Joshua's demand would then serve as an initial proof of the state of their hearts and of their intention to be faithful to the covenant.

For the third time, the Israelites swear a public oath that they will serve God alone and obey him alone (see 24:18,21). Israel's oath of allegiance to the covenant with the Lord is thus clear and emphatic. It is a final, conclusive, solemn declaration on their part.

Statement of display (24:25–26a)

Many ancient Near-Eastern covenants include a written statement for public display. The words of the treaty are written down as a confirmation that the covenant has been established and agreed to by both parties. One example is found in Deuteronomy 27:1–4.

When the Israelites cross the Jordan River into the promised land, then they are to erect a series of large stones, coat them with lime plaster and write on them the words of the covenant document that has been given to them. These are to serve as a symbol and a reminder of the covenant promises and duties.[5]

Some Hittite treaties are inscribed on tablets for these very purposes.[6]

In the present episode, Joshua writes down the words of the covenant renewal 'in the Book of the Law of God'. The nature of this document is a matter of debate. The precise title, 'the Book of the Law of God', is found elsewhere in the Bible only in Nehemiah 8:18. There it clearly refers to the Mosaic law (see, also Nehemiah 8:1,3). On the basis of that reference some commentators argue that Joshua is actually writing in the Torah (and cf. Deuteronomy 31:26). Thus, the assumption is that the Torah (the five books of Moses) had not been completed before Joshua's time, and that Joshua is simply adding to it. Another option is that this book is a stand-alone treaty document that has been lost to posterity. A third possibility is that the writing referred to is actually an inscription on the stone of witness that Joshua erects at Shechem (cf. Deuteronomy 27:1–4).

A second witness (24:26b–28)

Joshua then sets up a large standing stone at Shechem. This stone is to serve as a second 'witness' to the covenantal agreement and to the sanctions that follow from obedience or disobedience (24:27).

> Holding a treaty renewal here may have been a polemic against Canaanite beliefs; Shechem was the site of the temple of Baal-berith (Judges 9:4), a pagan god whose name meant 'lord of the covenant'. The sense of the ritual for Israel was to underscore that only the LORD was the true Lord of the covenant.[7]

Archaeologists have uncovered a standing stone in the temple of Baal-berith at Shechem that may, in fact, be Joshua's stone of witness.

The text says that the stone is a witness, 'for it has heard all the words of the LORD that he spoke to us'. This is an odd, almost eerie, expression. It is not that Joshua has some type of 'primitive animistic hangover',[8] but he is employing the figure of speech known as personification. Although the stone is inanimate, it symbolically 'hears' and 'speaks' as a witness to the covenant.

This great stone is the seventh and final monument assembled by the people of God during the conquest and settlement of Canaan (see 4:20; 7:26; 8:28–29; 8:32; 10:27; 22:34). The number seven in Hebrew literature frequently symbolizes the concept of completion. In this case, Joshua's leadership, the general conquest and the settlement of the land have been completed.

Points to ponder

1. The oath of allegiance

At the very heart of the covenant at Shechem is the oath of allegiance taken by the Israelites. In fact, they make their pledge of obedience three times in the text. I have recently read the memoirs of Revelation John Livingstone, a Scottish divine of the seventeenth century. Livingstone was a member of the Westminster Assembly that met in the 1640s, while he pastored a church in Ireland. Within twenty years of the Assembly, some of the divines were thrown out of their churches due to the 'Great Ejectment' of 1662. They had refused to conform to the standards of the Church of England's *Book of Church Order*. Livingstone was brought before the ecclesiastical council in Edinburgh because of his refusal to conform.

Livingstone says:

> ... they required me to subserve [i.e. subscribe to] the oath which they called the Oath of Allegiance, wherein the king was to be acknowledged supreme governor over all persons, and in all causes, both civil and ecclesiastical. This I know was contrived ... that it might import [i.e. bring about] receding from the covenant for reformation, and the bringing in of the bishops... Therefore, I refused to take that oath. They desired to know if I would take some time to advise anent [i.e. to consider] the matter, as some who had been before them had done... I told I needed not take time, seeing I was abundantly clear that I could not lawfully take that oath.[9]

The ecclesiastical council pronounced banishment. Livingstone had forty-eight hours to leave Edinburgh and two months to depart from the king's domain altogether. He left his church and fled to Rotterdam. Within a year, his wife joined him with two of their children, although five children remained behind in Scotland. Livingstone, a lion of the Covenant, died in Rotterdam on 9 August 1672.

In my ordination examination, the first question I was asked was: 'Who is head of the church?' The answer is 'Jesus Christ alone.' That is the oath we are to take. Livingstone and others paid a heavy price for remaining true to that oath. Perhaps some day we too will be called upon to take our stand on that oath of allegiance.

2. Like Israel, our word must be our bond

Richard Cameron, one of those who had been exiled in the Great Ejectment, returned from Holland to Scotland in 1679. He did this in order to stand alongside the persecuted Covenanters in his land. In a sermon he preached in May 1680 he declared that much of Scotland acknowledged Charles II as their king, but declared, 'We will have no other king but Christ.' Cameron and some of his supporters were surrounded and massacred at Ayrsmoss. The enemy severed Cameron's head and hands, and affixed them to the Netherbow Port for all to see. And, indeed, all Scotland did see —and they said, 'There's the head and hands of a man who lived praying and preaching, and died praying and fighting.' Christ as King is an oath worth dying for!

3. Our God is a covenant-keeping God

The covenant is the very foundation and heart of Israel's existence. This is true for believers today as well. The covenant is certain, true and steadfast; we can rely unreservedly on our covenant-keeping God and his promises to us. How often in our lives there are times of ongoing trials—that is, hardships that never seem to go away. And how often we act as though there is no help, and as though we are left on our own to cope and to live! But we need to understand, as Bowes comments, that:

Amidst all the upheavings of a restless world, and all the errors of a distracted Church, the rock of truth remains steadfast for ever. The notions of men are constantly changing; the founders of systems pass away, but 'the foundation of God standeth sure'. The truth, the word, the promises, the covenant, of an unchanging God, are as sure as he is faithful.[10]

27

Three burials

Please read Joshua 24:29–33

The book of Joshua ends with three burials and obituaries. On the surface it all sounds despairing and hopeless. But, in reality, that is not the case at all. These three graves are memorials to the fulfilment of God's promise to give the land of Canaan to his people. Joseph longed to be buried in this land (Genesis 50:24–26) which God had promised to Abraham so long ago (Genesis 12:7). Joshua fought for this land, and now he is laid to rest in it. Eleazar had been the spiritual leader of the people during the last part of the wanderings, during the conquest and during the settlement. He was one of the leaders who allocated the land to the people, and now he too is buried in the land of promise.

The deaths of Joshua and Eleazar also mark the passing of the conquest generation; these two, the covenant mediator and the high priest, were the principal leaders of Israel during this time. A new generation of leadership will now take the reins of management in Israel. A question thus looms over this final episode of the book of Joshua: what will happen to Israel now that their leadership has died? This is the same question that weighed on the minds of the Israelites at the end of the book of Deuteronomy; Moses has died, and now what will happen to Israel?

Death and burial of Joshua (24:29–30)

This concluding section opens with the death of Joshua, the covenant mediator between God and Israel. For the first time in the book Joshua is given the title, 'the servant of the LORD'. This description was commonly used of Moses (see Deuteronomy 34:5), and it is often applied to him in the book of Joshua (1:1; 8:31,33; 11:12; 12:6; 13:8; etc.). The use of this title serves as an *inclusio,* or a bracket, for the entire book. The first verse of the book tells of the death of Moses, 'the servant of the LORD', and here at the close of the book we find the narration of the death of Joshua, 'the servant of the LORD'. What a fitting epitaph for these two covenant mediators and leaders of the people of God!

Joshua dies at the ripe age of 110 years. This is the same age that Joseph was when he died in Egypt (Genesis 50:22). The Egyptians viewed this figure as the ideal lifespan.[1] This demonstrates that God blesses and favours Joshua for the rest of his life. Joshua is further commended by being buried in 'his own inheritance', which had been deeded to him in Joshua 19:49–50. He received his promised possession in the land of Canaan, and that is where his body is entombed!

Serving the Lord (24:31)

This is a summary comment that describes Israel's fidelity to the Lord and to the covenant. It is important to note that there is a time restriction on this devotion and obedience: the Israelites serve the Lord faithfully during the life of Joshua and the lives of the elders of his day who outlive him. The verse is ominous because it anticipates a time when Israel will not serve the Lord. That time will come quickly.

The next generation lives in the period of the judges. Judges 2:11-19 describes this time as one of great apostasy. It is an era of cyclical history with regard to Israel's unfaithfulness to the covenant: the Israelites begin by serving other gods (vv. 11-13); God responds in anger and he delivers them into the hands of their enemies (vv. 14-15); the people then cry out to the Lord and he raises up a judge to deliver them (v. 16); the judge succeeds for a short time, but Israel quickly returns to idolatry (v. 17). It is important to observe also that the people not only revert to their wicked ways after each deliverance, but that they become more corrupt than they were before (vv. 18-19). Thus the book of Judges reflects a downward spiral of Israel into apostasy. What a contrast to Joshua's generation, as described in Joshua 24:31!

Certainly one reason that Israel kept the covenant during Joshua's generation is that their leadership 'had known all the work that the LORD did for Israel'. In other words, the elders of Israel did not have a mere head knowledge about God's work in the conquest and settlement of the land; rather, they truly experienced it. The verb 'to know' can often bear the idea of an intimate, personal knowledge, understanding and experience. These leaders had seen the great works of the Lord, and that experience encouraged them to keep faithful to the covenant.

The bones of Joseph (24:32)
At the close of the book of Genesis, Joseph made the Israelites promise that they would bring up his bones from Egypt to

Canaan when the people were delivered by God out of Egypt (Genesis 50:24–25). This promise is now fulfilled at the end of the book of Joshua, at least four hundred years after the oath had been taken.

Burial in the land of Canaan appears to have been very important to the Hebrews (see, for example, 1 Samuel 31:11–13; 2 Samuel 21:12–14), and especially the preservation of a person's bones (see 1 Kings 13:29–31; 2 Kings 23:16–20). Interment in the land of promise may be in anticipation of a resurrection there (2 Kings 13:20–21; Ezekiel 37:1–14). Joseph himself may have believed in the bodily resurrection of the dead (Hebrews 11:17–22).[2]

This verse ends by saying, literally, 'And *they* became an inheritance of the descendants of Joseph.' To whom or what does 'they' refer? Some commentators argue that it can only refer back grammatically to the antecedent 'sons of Hamor', which must then be understood as referring to the plot of land that Jacob bought from them.[3] In reality, the 'they' may refer to the bones of Joseph. In a sense, then, the bones of Joseph become an 'inheritance', or 'possession' of the sons of Joseph. They are, in other words, a legacy or a heritage for the two tribes of Ephraim and Manasseh. By this bequest the two tribes are continually reminded of their past history; as they settle into the land of Canaan, their presence there is a fulfilment of the desires and hopes of the patriarch Joseph.

Death of burial of Eleazar (24:33)

Eleazar was installed as high priest in place of his father Aaron during the wilderness wanderings (Numbers 20:22–29). He is a prominent figure in the Pentateuch (Exodus 6:23–25; Leviticus 10; Numbers 19:3–4, etc.) and in the book of Joshua (14:1; 17:4;

21:1). He now dies, and he is buried in Gibeah. This town had apparently been deeded to Phinehas, the son of Eleazar, during the allotment of Canaan to Israel. Phinehas is the grandson of Aaron, and he now becomes high priest of Israel (Judges 20:27–28).

Points to ponder

1. Our hope is in the Lord, not in men

Although the leadership of Israel dies, yet the Lord lives for ever and ever. Israel's leaders are weak, broken, tired and mortal, but the Lord is tireless, omnipotent, pure and eternal. And so Israel's true hope and strength is the Lord. As the psalmist declares:

I lift up my eyes to the hills.
   From where does my help come?
My help comes from the LORD,
   who made heaven and earth.
He will not let your foot be moved;
   he who keeps you will not slumber.
Behold, he who keeps Israel
   will neither slumber nor sleep

(Psalm 121:1–4).

The church today is in the same circumstances as ancient Israel: our great leaders die and go to their eternal rest. But we ought to be encouraged, even in such dire situations as those, because the hope of the church and its continuing existence are not ultimately dependent on men but on the Lord. I once had an elderly, godly pastor say to me, 'When I look to men I am discouraged, but when I look to Christ I am encouraged.' Men pass from this earth:

Time, like an ever-rolling stream,
Bears all its sons away;
They fly forgotten, as a dream
Dies at the op'ning day.[4]

But the Lord remains for ever! As the nineteenth-century hymn so eloquently states, 'The church's one foundation is Jesus Christ, her Lord.'

2. The hope of the resurrection
Joseph anticipated the bodily resurrection of the dead for God's people.

He gave directions concerning his bones because he believed that God could raise men even from the dead. Jesus Christ is the fulfilment of what Joseph merely anticipated. He taught, 'Do not marvel at this; for an hour is coming, in which all who are in the tombs will hear his voice, and will come forth; those who did the good deeds to a resurrection of life, those who committed the evil deeds to a resurrection of judgement' (John 5:28–29). The first-fruits of his work occurred at the event of the crucifixion: 'And behold, the veil of the temple was torn in two from top to bottom; and the earth shook and the rocks were split. The tombs were opened, and many bodies of the saints who had fallen asleep were raised; and coming out of the tombs after his resurrection they entered the holy city and appeared to many' (Matthew 27:51–53). Those many saints raised from the dead are a sign to us of a final resurrection, when believers will be raised to eternal life with Christ, and unbelievers to eternal death. Oh to be part of the resurrection that leads to life![5]

When all is said and done, death is not the end for the true people of God. It is merely the gate to the eternal inheritance that is 'imperishable, undefiled, and unfading' (1 Peter 1:4).

Notes

Introduction

1. J. Milgrom, *Numbers,* JPS Torah Commentary (Philadelphia: Jewish Publication Society, 1990), p.xiii.

2. R. Alter, *The Art of Biblical Narrative* (New York: Basic Books, 1981), p.12.

3. The ESV omits the word 'voice', although *qol* is in the original text.

4. R. B. Chisholm, *Interpreting the Historical Books* (Grand Rapids: Kregel, 2006), p.228.

5. H. J. Koorevaar, *De Opbouw van het Boek Jozua,* Diss. Theol. (Leuven: University of Brussels, 1990).

Chapter 1—Be strong and courageous (1:1–9)

1. See the account in W. G. Blaikie, *The Preachers of Scotland* (Edinburgh: Banner of Truth, reprinted 2001), pp.118–19.

2. While some archaeologists argue that the Late Bronze Age has very few

fortifications in Canaan, this is probably untrue. At numerous sites, the huge fortifications of the Middle Bronze period were reused and rebuilt during the Late Bronze Age.

3. N. Sarna, *Genesis,* JPS Torah Commentary (Philadelphia: Jewish Publication Society, 1989), p.100.

4. J. Niehaus, *God at Sinai: Covenant and Theophany in the Bible and Ancient Near East* (Grand Rapids: Zondervan, 1995), p.175.

Chapter 2—Joshua takes command (1:10–18)

1. J. Blanchard, *The Complete Gathered Gold* (Darlington: Evangelical Press, 2006), p.432.

2. Ibid. p.212.

3. J. Purves, *Fair Sunshine: Character Studies of the Scottish Covenanters* (Edinburgh: Banner of Truth, 1968), pp.50–51.

4. Ibid. p.51.

5. J. Flavel, *The Works of John Flavel,* vol. iv (London: Banner of Truth, 1968), p.519.

6. J. Currid, *Why Do I Suffer? Suffering and the Sovereignty of God* (Ross-shire: Christian Focus, 2004), p.114.

7. J. Currid, *A Study Commentary on Numbers* (Darlington: Evangelical Press, 2009), p.408.

8. Ibid. p.408.

9. D. R. Davis, *Joshua: No Falling Words* (Grand Rapids: Baker, 1988), p.21.

Chapter 3—Reconnoitring the land (2:1–24)

1. E. F. Campbell, 'The Amarna Letters and the Amarna Period,' *Biblical Archaeologist* 23:1 (1960), pp.2–22.

2. Ibid. p.22.

3. T. O. Lambdin, *Introduction to Biblical Hebrew* (New York: Scribner's, 1971), p.168.

4. See M. Coogan, ed., *Stories from Ancient Canaan* (Philadelphia: Westminster, 1978).

5. A. Mazar, *Archaeology of the Land of the Bible* (New York: Doubleday, 1990), pp.386–8.

6. J. Currid, *A Study Commentary on Exodus*, vol. 1 (Darlington: Evangelical Press, 2000), p.244.

7. This verb is a perfect in Hebrew, which indicates completed action.

8. Thomas Vincent, *God's Terrible Voice in the City* (Morgan, PA: Soli Deo Gloria Publications, 1997 reprint), pp.37–8.

9. Ibid. p.50.

Chapter 4—Dividing of the Jordan River (3:1–17)

1. F. Brown, S. R. Driver and C. A. Briggs, *A Hebrew and English Lexicon of the Old Testament* (Oxford: Clarendon Press, 1975 reprint), p.386.

2. The word translated 'officers' is a broad term that is used of judicial, civil,

or military leaders; that the last group is what is intended is confirmed by Joshua 1:10, which uses the same word to speak of military personnel.

3. J. Currid, *A Study Commentary on Deuteronomy* (Darlington: Evangelical Press, 2007), p.180.

Chapter 6—The final act at the Jordan River (4:11–24)

1. Faith Cook, *Fearless Pilgrim: The Life and Times of John Bunyan* (Darlington: Evangelical Press, 2008), p.358.

2. John Bunyan, 'A Treatise on the Fear of God,' in *The Desire of the Righteous Granted; The Works of John Bunyan,* ed. G. Offor (Edinburgh: Banner of Truth, 1991), p.485.

Chapter 7—Setting one's house into proper spiritual order (5:1–12)

1. R. Brown, *The Message of Numbers* (Downers Grove, IL: Inter-Varsity, 2002), p.71.

Chapter 8—The fall of Jericho (5:13–6:27)

1. See Currid, *Exodus,* vol. 1, p.81.

2. G. K. Beale, *The Temple and the Church's Mission* (Downer's Grove, IL: InterVarsity, 2004), pp.63–4.

3. J. Pritchard, ed., *Ancient Near Eastern Texts Relating to the Old Testament* (Princeton: Princeton University Press, 3rd edition, 1969), p.320.

4. See Currid, *Why Do I Suffer?,* pp.36–41.

5. See J. Appleby, *I Can Plod: William Carey and the Early Years of the First Baptist Missionary Society* (London: Grace Publications, 2007).

Chapter 9—Defeat at Ai (7:1-26)

1. Jeremiah Burroughs, *A Treatise on Earthly-Mindedness,* Soli Deo Gloria Ministries, reprinted 1997.

2. Interestingly, in the original Hebrew of this verse the criminal is not called Achan but Achor. The verse literally reads, 'The son of Carmi: Achor, the Achor of Israel...'

Chapter 10—Defeat of Ai (8:1-29)

1. Currid, *Exodus,* vol. I, pp. 366-7.

2. Patrick Johnstone, *Operation World* (Carlisle, UK: Paternoster Press, 2001), pp.15-16.

Chapter 11—Covenant renewal (8:30-35)

1. Davis, *Joshua: No Falling Words,* p.72.

2. Thomas Guthrie, *The Way to Life* (New York: Robert Carter, 1873), p.91.

3. Currid, *Deuteronomy,* p.424.

4. Ibid. p.423.

5. J. C. Ryle, *Practical Religion* (Cambridge: J. Clark, 1970 reprint), p.88.

6. J. C. Ryle, *Expository Thoughts on the Gospel of Mark* (Carlisle, PA: Banner of Truth, 2000 reprint), comments on Mark 12:18-27.

Chapter 12—Covenant with the Gibeonites (9:1–27)

1. Gibeon is located at the modern site of el-Jib. Excavations at the site have uncovered thirty-one jar handles inscribed with the name *gb'n*, and they confirm the identification of Gibeon with el-Jib.

2. M. Wouldstra, *The Book of Joshua,* NICOT (Grand Rapids: Eerdmans, 1981), p.159.

3. Currid, *Deuteronomy,* p.456.

4. Davis, *Joshua: No Falling Words,* p.78.

Chapter 13—The battle against the five kings (10:1–27)

1. Pritchard, ed., *Ancient Near Eastern Texts,* p.204.

2. Davis, *Joshua: No Falling Words,* pp.84–6.

3. Currid, *Exodus,* vol. 1, p.300.

4. Davis, *Joshua: No Falling Words,* p.86.

5. Currid, *Exodus,* vol. 1, p.235.

6. Currid, *Deuteronomy,* p.357.

7. E. M. Bounds, *Power through Prayer* (CreateSpace, 2009 reprint), p.1.

Chapter 14—The southern campaign (10:28–43)

1. J. Niehaus, 'Pa'am 'Ehat and the Israelite Conquest,' *Vetus Testamentum* 30 (1980), p.238; cf. Davis, *Joshua: No Falling Words,* pp.88–9.

Chapter 15—*The northern campaign (11:1–23)*

1. A. W. Pink, *The Attributes of God* (Grand Rapids: Baker, 1988 edition), p.31.

2. John Calvin, *Institutes,* trans. H. Beveridge (Grand Rapids: Eerdmans, 1981 reprint), I, xvi, 179.

3. Currid, *Exodus,* vol. 1, p.114.

4. Currid, *Why do I suffer?,* p.23.

5. E. B. Pusey, *Parochial Sermons* (Oxford: John Henry Parker, 1853), vol. 2, p.93.

Chapter 16—*Summary of the conquest (12:1–24)*

1. Wouldstra, *The Book of Joshua,* p.200.

2. The Hebrew word the ESV translates as 'valley' can also mean 'river'. It is used this way in verse 2 of the present text with regard to 'the river Jabbok'.

3. Pritchard, ed., *Ancient Near Eastern Texts,* pp. 231–64.

Chapter 17—*Distribution of the land east of the Jordan (13:1–33)*

1. Currid, *Numbers,* p.311.

2. A. Bennett, ed., *The Valley of Vision: A Collection of Puritan Prayers and Devotions* (Edinburgh: Banner of Truth, 1975), p.44.

Chapter 18—*Introduction to the distribution of the land west of the Jordan (14:1–15)*

1. Currid, *Numbers,* p.365.

Chapter 19—Judah's allotment (15:1-63)

1. Davis, *Joshua: No Falling Words,* p.123.

2. J. Calvin, *Commentaries on the Book of Joshua* (Grand Rapids: Baker, 1993 reprint), p.206.

3. Wouldstra, *The Book of Joshua,* p.243.

4. This point is evidence that the book of Joshua was written prior to the United Monarchy.

5. A. Hoekema, *The Bible and the Future* (Grand Rapids: Eerdmans, 1979), p.274.

Chapter 20—Allotment for the tribes of Joseph (16:1-17:18)

1. John D. Currid and David P. Barrett, *The Crossway ESV Bible Atlas* (Wheaton: Crossway, 2010), p.138.

2. Currid, *Numbers,* p.368.

Chapter 21—The remaining allotments (18:1-19:51)

1. J. Currid, *A Study Commentary on Leviticus* (Darlington: Evangelical Press, 2004), p.13.

2. See Currid and Barrett, *The Crossway ESV Bible Atlas.*

3. J. Currid, *A Study Commentary on Genesis,* vol. 2 (Darlington: Evangelical Press, 2003), p.381.

4. Wouldstra, *The Book of Joshua,* pp.270-71.

5. Ibid. pp. 270–71.

Chapter 22—Cities of refuge (20:1–9)

1. Currid, *Numbers,* p.439.

2. Excavations of Iron Age city gates in Israel, such as at the site of Gezer, have revealed that many of these gate complexes have seating areas built into them.

3. R. K. Harrison, *Numbers: An Exegetical Commentary* (Grand Rapids: Baker, 1992), p.422.

4. Davis, *Joshua: No Falling Words,* p.152.

5. Currid, *Numbers,* pp.442–3.

Chapter 23—Levitical cities and pasture lands (21:1–45)

1. K. Gutbrod, *Das Buch vom Landes Gottes* (Stuttgart: Calwer, 1951).

2. Currid, *Deuteronomy,* p.318.

3. R. Baxter, *The Saints' Everlasting Rest* (New York: Revell, 1962 edition), p.29.

4. Ibid. p.181.

Chapter 24—The altar (22:1–34)

1. See, for example, J. R. Sizoo, 'The Book of Joshua: Exposition,' *The Interpreter's Bible,* 12 vols. (New York: Abingdon, 1953), vol. 2, p.658.

2. Augustine, *Contra lit. Petil.,* I, xxix, n. 31.

3. J. Currid, *A Study Commentary on Exodus,* vol. 2 (Darlington: Evangelical Press, 2001), p.60.

4. Guthrie, *The Way to Life,* p.91.

Chapter 25—Joshua's charge (23:1–16)

1. *ESV Study Bible,* p.428.

2. The verb 'to cling' is also used of the fidelity that is foundational to the monogamous marriage relationship declared in Genesis 2:24.

Chapter 26—Second renewal of the covenant (24:1–28)

1. Currid, *Deuteronomy,* p.13.

2. M. G. Kline, *Treaty of the Great King: The Covenant Structure of Deuteronomy* (Grand Rapids: Eerdmans, 1963), p.50.

3. Currid, *Deuteronomy,* p.38.

4. Pritchard, ed., *Ancient Near Eastern Texts,* pp. 203–5.

5. Currid, *Deuteronomy,* p.17.

6. Pritchard, ed., *Ancient Near Eastern Texts,* p.205.

7. Currid and Barrett, *The Crossway ESV Bible Atlas,* pp.103–4.

8. Davis, *Joshua: No Falling Words,* p.203.

9. The spelling has been modernized.

10. George Seaton Bowes, *Scripture Itself the Illustrator* (London: James Nesbit, 1872), p.126.

Chapter 27—Three burials (24:29–33)

1. J. Vergote, *Joseph en Egypte* (Louvain: Publications Universitaires, 1959), pp.200–201.

2. Currid, *Genesis,* vol. 2, p.401.

3. See, for instance, Wouldstra, *Joshua,* p.361, n. 8.

4. Isaac Watts, 'Our God, Our Help in Ages Past' (1719).

5. Currid, *Genesis,* vol. 2, p.402.